Understanding God's
ETERNAL
Plan for Israel

Deby Brown

ISBN: 978-1-4834-7506-6 (sc)
ISBN: 978-1-4834-7507-3 (e)

Library of Congress Control Number: 2017914003

Because of the dynamic nature of the Internet, any web addresses or links contained in this book may have changed since publication and may no longer be valid. The views expressed in this work are solely those of the author and do not necessarily reflect the views of the publisher, and the publisher hereby disclaims any responsibility for them.

Unless otherwise indicated, Scripture was taken from the New King James Version®. Copyright © 1982 by Thomas Nelson. Used by permission. All rights reserved.

Scripture quotations marked (NIV) are taken from the Holy Bible, New International Version®, NIV®. Copyright © 1973, 1978, 1984, 2011 by Biblica, Inc.™ Used by permission of Zondervan. All rights reserved worldwide. www.zondervan.com The "NIV" and "New International Version" are trademarks registered in the United States Patent and Trademark Office by Biblica, Inc.™

Scripture quotations are from the ESV® Bible (The Holy Bible, English Standard Version®), copyright © 2001 by Crossway, a publishing ministry of Good News Publishers. Used by permission. All rights reserved.

Scripture taken from the Holy Bible: International Standard Version®. Copyright © 1996-forever by The ISV Foundation. ALL RIGHTS RESERVED INTERNATIONALLY. Used by permission.

Scripture quotations taken from the New American Standard Bible® (NASB), Copyright © 1960, 1962, 1963, 1968, 1971, 1972, 1973, 1975, 1977, 1995 by The Lockman Foundation Used by permission. www.Lockman.org

Author Photo by Julia Humphrey.
All sketches provided with permission by Ray Hart, 2017.
All photos provided with permission by Thomas Winder and Deby Brown, 2017.

Lulu Publishing Services rev. date: 10/25/2017

CONTENTS

Part One
Biblical Israel

Part Four
Spiritual Israel

FOREWORD

Born of a deep and abiding love for God's chosen people, Israel, Deby Brown passionately makes the case that God has plans for Israel in His redemption of mankind. If you love Israel, read this book. If you *don't* love Israel, read this book.

—Pete De Lacy, Vice President of Content,
Precept Ministries International

In "Understanding God's Eternal Plan for Israel," Deby Brown gives the reader a good overview of the theological and historical importance of modern day Israel. She is a teacher at heart and wholeheartedly tackles daunting and complex issues in order to simplify and explain them to a Christian audience. This volume is commended for its contribution in mobilizing Christians to pray for and support the Jewish state.

—Susan Michael, USA Director, International
Christian Embassy Jerusalem

If there is an important historical and political national issue in the world today, it is the establishment of the State of Modern Israel in 1948. Even though it is a small nation state, about the geographical size of the State of New Jersey, it is an economic powerhouse producing high technology and agricultural products for many other nations of the world. Any person with an iPhone carries and uses Israeli technology daily.

Author Deby Brown has described vividly both the biblical and historical roots of Israel. In her first section on "Biblical Israel" she portrays what the Bible says historically and prophetically about the past and future of Israel. The four biblical covenants (Abrahamic, Mosaic, New & Davidic) describe in such a dramatic way God's plan for the future of Israel. In a parallel manner, Deby Brown presents the modern historical issues regarding what has taken and is taking place in the Middle East. Past and present national conquerors are similar in their desire to control that important corridor of land in the eastern Mediterranean.

I strongly recommend this book for the modern reader!
—George Giacumakis, Ph.D. Professor of History, California State University, Fullerton; Director of The Museum of Biblical & Sacred Writings; and "Director of HistoryOnTheMove Study Tours to the Middle East and the Mediterranean areas.

On an intellectual quest, back in 1984, to follow the footsteps of Jesus; traveling from Upper Egypt to Central Turkey, something unexpected took place. In the depths of my soul a light grew from a dim twinkle to a towering flame. I discovered the wealth of truth and history found in the many books of the Bible. Stories once read as mere fables or myth, became as real as the air I breathed. It was time for me to "first seek His Kingdom, and His righteousness, and not worry about selfish ambition".

The Word says that truth will set one free. Consequently, my preconceived beliefs, formed from childhood, also went through visible transformation. Two seminaries, multiple degrees, eight years on staff at Trinity Southwest University, (a non-denominational Seminary), and now a Biblical Archaeologist; what is undeniable, is that the "Church" has a horrible past of antisemitism. Unfortunately, the disgraceful history of persecution of the Jewish people is squarely placed on the shoulders of the Church. From Emperor Constantine to Saint Augustine and even the great protestor, Martin Luther; one common thread was agreed on, that Jews were to blame for the death of Jesus, therefore, God must be finished with the Jewish people and that God's eternal covenants with them are null and void. Apparently, it didn't matter what the Bible said, or what the truth was; for some of the worst atrocities known to man have been committed against the Jewish people, all too often, in the name of the Cross. What happened to "Love thy neighbor?"

Finally, "Understanding Gods Eternal Plan for Israel," by Deby Brown, answers these sensitive questions and provides the reader with the Biblical mandates to follow concerning our treatment of Israel and the Jewish people. A must read for understanding the past, present, and future for the most important land on Earth. God's own land, the State of Israel.

—Rev. Thomas Winder, Executive Director "Church of the Transfiguration Restoration Project, Maj dal Shams, Israel. Brother Thomas Ministries, 7601 Keith Ct SW, Albuquerque, New Mexico, 87105.

Deby Brown's book, "God's Plan for Israel" is a must for any serious Christian. The book follows several themes including a deeper look at four of God's sacred covenants, Christian responsibilities towards Israel and the Jewish people, and two very disturbing trends – the Boycotts, Divestment, and Sanctions (BDS) movement, and replacement theology. A well-informed Christian needs to know his or her Bible and history, as well as emerging trends within our society and the Church.

I commend Deby for tackling such challenging topics, while keeping them interesting and contemporary.

—Robb Schwartz, author of "Operation Last Exodus," a book on the possibility of another holocaust in the United States, and the final return of the Jewish people to their ancient homeland. Robb writes and lectures in Orange County, California. www.operationlastexodus.com

PREFACE

Israel is the most hotly-discussed news topic around the world. There is no other nation or people group in history that have experienced what Israel has. Throughout history, time and time again, people and nations have tried to destroy the Jewish people. With anti-Semitism on the rise once more and enemies threatening to wipe Israel from the face of the earth, many Christians want instead to show their love for Israel and the Jewish people. However, most Christians have no idea how to show support for or how to defend the Jewish people. To stand with Israel, one must understand their history, their spiritual background, the political issues they face today and God's forever promises to them. God says He has written His name on Jerusalem, claims it is the place He Himself will dwell at the end of the age, and refers to it as the apple of His eye. This is why *Understanding God's Eternal Plan For Israel* was written.

As founder and president of *Song For Israel*, our goal is to proclaim God's eternal plan for Israel. I hope you will enjoy reading this book and that it will not only help you understand your roots in the Jewish faith but also help you gain a greater love and understanding of your Jewish friends and neighbors.

If you are Jewish, I hope and pray that as you read this book, you will come to know there are multitudes of believers in Jesus Christ (Yeshua the Messiah) who love you and would give their lives to stand with you. Yeshua *did* give His life for you and He loves you. Forever.

For Zion's sake I will not keep silent,
And for Jerusalem's sake I will not keep quiet,
Until her righteousness goes forth like brightness,
And her salvation like a torch that is burning.
Isaiah 62:1 (NASB)

PART ONE

Biblical Israel

CHAPTER 1

God's Plan versus Satan's Plan

God has a stated eternal plan for you and for me, as well as for Israel. To understand God's plan, one needs to understand the beginning and end of time as we know it and how we and Israel fit into it.

The Beginning—Before Time

Time did not begin with the creation of earth in Genesis 1:1. It began earlier and is spoken of in Ephesians 1:4–5—"He [God] chose us in Him before the foundation of the world, that we should be holy and without blame before Him in love, having predestined us to adoption as sons by Jesus Christ to Himself, according to the good pleasure of His will."

If God is infallible, then we can rightly assume that His Word is also infallible. God wrote His plan down in His Book, called the Holy Bible, which He says is infallible, meaning not capable of error:

- Prophets are completely reliable; they spoke from God as they heard from the Holy Spirit—2 Peter 1:19–21
- All Scripture is God-breathed—2 Timothy 3:16–17
- The law of the LORD is perfect—Psalm 19:7
- The statutes of the LORD are right—Psalm 19:8

God and His Word are so closely related that John 1:14 says "the Word became flesh and dwelt among us, and we beheld His glory, the glory as of the only begotten of the Father, full of grace and truth."

God's Plan

God selected a nation through which to work out His plan to bring salvation to the world (Deuteronomy 7:6–8). This nation would be a light to the world (Isaiah 49:6), a holy priesthood (Exodus 19:6), and the apple of His eye (Zechariah 2:8). The nation God chose is Israel.

The promises of God were given to the Jewish people (Exodus 19:5, Deuteronomy 7:6–8, Romans 3:2). God promised to protect them through the ages. Through the Jewish people God would bring His message of eternal salvation to the world.

Israel is unique in that no other nation has been given the role that God has given them—Israel alone has been appointed as the custodian of the Word of God. If Israel were to fail (and she won't—God would not allow that), then God's plan for world redemption would fail. God guarantees Israel's survival.

God has said that we are to bless Israel. In fact, God's Word says that if we bless Israel, He will bless us. Likewise, if we curse Israel, He will curse us (Genesis 12:3).

Satan's Plan

Satan was also known as Lucifer (Isaiah 14:12), an angel in heaven. He was beautiful—In Ezekiel 28:12–15, God describes Lucifer as He compares him to the sinful king of Tyre:

> "You were the seal of perfection, full of wisdom and perfect in beauty. You were in Eden, the garden of God; every precious stone was your covering: the sardius, topaz, and diamond, beryl, onyx, and jasper, sapphire, turquoise, and emerald with gold. The workmanship of your timbrels and

pipes was prepared for you on the day you were created. You
were the anointed cherub who covers; I established you;
You were on the holy mountain of God; You walked back
and forth in the midst of fiery stones. You were perfect in
your ways from the day you were created, till iniquity was
found in you."

God referred to Lucifer as the "anointed cherub," giving him the highest
created position. No other angel was created with the beauty and intelligence
that God gave to him.

But before the creation of Earth, Lucifer planned to usurp God and His
plan. We know this because Lucifer had already fallen from heaven before
he met Eve in the garden to tempt her (Genesis 3:1–7).

How you are fallen from heaven, O Lucifer, son of the morning! How you are cut down to the ground, you who weakened the nations! For you have said in your heart: "I will ascend into heaven, I will exalt my throne above the stars of God; I will also sit on the mount of the congregation on the farthest sides of the north; I will ascend above the heights of the clouds, I will be like the Most High." (Isaiah 14:12–14)

What was Lucifer's plan to usurp God and His plan? How might Satan be exalted above the stars of God and be like God? He would have to overthrow God's plan. Satan has been the head of the evil world system and the power behind the evil rulers in history. He has used earthly kings and rulers to accomplish his plan through them.

Satan is the principality behind the powers of this corrupt world system. According to 2 Corinthians 11:14–15, Satan transforms himself into an angel of light. Likewise, his "ministers" (those who serve him) look like they rule with righteousness, but they will get their just rewards in the end.

> For we do not wrestle against flesh and blood, but against principalities; against powers, against the rulers of the darkness of this age, against spiritual hosts of wickedness in the heavenly places.
> —Ephesians 6:12

The Battle Begins

Once God stated His plan for world redemption using Israel as His vehicle, Satan put his own plan into action to usurp God's plan and destroy Israel. Satan has thrown in every roadblock, every evil scheme and deception, to foil God's plan. Time and again, Satan has caused nations and people groups to come against God's chosen people. Often it looked as though the Jewish people would be annihilated, but God has always protected a remnant.

The Battle Continues ...

Satan challenged the very role that God assigned to Israel—and He continues to come against the Most High God. When you understand the plan of God versus the plan of Satan, you can understand why the world has come against the tiny nation of Israel and the Jewish people around the world.

The plan of God will not fail. When you study prophetic scriptures, you will see how the plans and promises of God have been or are being fulfilled.

The Battle Will Not End Until the Prince of Peace Comes

Scripture teaches that there will be an end to Satan and his rule over the earth. God will ultimately have His way and restore the earth and His people to the place He intended in the Garden of Eden.

In the chapters ahead, you will discover that God has revealed His plan for the world through His covenants. He has explained to us His desire for the type of relationship Gentiles should have with the Jews. You will gain an understanding of the biblical holidays as they reveal God's eternal plan for Israel. You

> All who knew you [Satan] among the peoples are astonished at you; you have become a horror, and shall be no more forever—Ezekiel 28:19.

will see the history of Israel in a nutshell and understand why many Jewish people do not trust Christians. You will see how the Middle East conflicts began and where it stands today. Most importantly, you will be warned of a disturbing trend in the churches of today—teaching the replacement of Israel with the Church as the new chosen people of God.

The battle against Israel is not just a physical battle but a spiritual battle. Satan's evil plan began before time and will not end until the Prince of Peace comes in all His glory to save the earth and bring permanent peace.

CHAPTER 2

Three Reasons Many Jewish People Do Not Trust in Jesus

> The primary reason Jewish people will not easily consider the possibility that Jesus is the Messiah is because of the historically negative relationship Jewish people have had with Christianity.
>
> —Mitch Glaser, Chosen People Ministries

Does that quote shock you? After reading this chapter, you will agree.

Before discussing the reasons for Jewish people's distrust of Jesus, there are a few important things we as Christians need to understand.

Some believe that Jewish people can get to heaven by keeping the Old Testament laws. However, remember that the purpose of the Law was to be a tutor pointing to Jesus (Yeshua is the Hebrew name for Jesus). No one can *keep* the Law—faith in Christ *saves* us from the Law. (For further explanation of this, see "New Covenant" in Chapter 3.)

Dual covenant is a doctrine that teaches there are two ways to find salvation—one for the Jewish people (through the Law) and one for everyone else (through the cross of Yeshua). If the first were true, then John 14:6 would not make any sense: "Jesus said ... 'I am the way, the truth, and the life. No one comes to the Father except through Me." The Word of God is clear that there is only *one* way to the Father—not through the Law, but through Christ.

Believers are reluctant to share the gospel with their Jewish friends, believing it's not important because Romans 11:26 says "all Israel will be saved." Some Christians believe God will save the Jewish people regardless. However, this reference is for the future. The Scriptures point to a time when all Jewish people will see firsthand the miracles of God. He will draw them *all* to Himself. Until then, Jewish people are perishing without the truth of God's Word which is for *them* as much as it is for you and me. Jesus clearly stated to Thomas, His Jewish follower, in John 14:6, "I am the way, the truth, and the life. No one comes to the Father except through Me."

Why is it so difficult for the Jewish people to believe in the Messiah? There are three reasons, among many, which stand out.

Reason 1: God has Partially Blinded the Jewish People

One of the saddest stories in the Bible is the story of the Jewish people rejecting their own Messiah. After waiting for and anticipating His arrival, most Jewish people did not recognize Him. The Jews of Jesus's time had studied the Old Testament Scriptures and believed the Messiah was supposed to be a political leader who would expel their enemies from their territory, re-establish the primacy of the Jewish nation, and bring peace and prosperity back to God's chosen people.

But that is not why Jesus came. Although the prophecies of political peace are yet to be fulfilled during the thousand-year reign of Christ, His purpose on earth was to bring personal peace (salvation) between people and God. Even more shocking, that peace was to be offered to the Gentiles just as freely as to the Jews.

Here are some statistics that may be of interest: In May 2017, there were 8.6 million people living in Israel, approximately 6.4 million of them ethnically Jewish.[1] Of the 6.4 million, 20,000 were Messianic Jews (that is, those who believe Jesus is the Messiah), which is less than half of one percent (0.31 percent).

---

[1] "Vital Statistics: Latest Population Statistics for Israel," Jewish Virtual Library, updated May 2017, http://www.jewishvirtuallibrary.org/latest-population-statistics-for-israel.

In May 2017, there were 7.5 billion people worldwide, of which 13.8 million were ethnically Jewish[2]. Of those 13.8 million, only 500,000 were Jewish believers, at 3.62 percent. This means there are 13.3 million Jewish "pre-believers" (not yet followers of Yeshua) in the world!

What does Scripture teach us about this partial blinding? John 12:40 says, "He [God] has blinded their eyes and hardened their hearts." Why did God blind them? The verses previous to John 12:40 answer that question. God blinded them because Jesus came to the Jewish people and did signs and wonders in front of them, yet they rejected Him as Messiah.

How long will the blinding last? Paul tells us:

> For I do not desire, brethren, that you should be ignorant of this mystery, lest you should be wise in your own opinion, that hardening in part has happened to Israel until the fullness of the Gentiles has come in. And so all Israel will be saved, as it is written: 'The Deliverer will come out of Zion, and He will turn away ungodliness from Jacob; for this is My covenant with them, when I take away their sins." (Romans 11:25–26)

The blinders will be removed and all Israel will be saved.

Reason 2: Christians Have Persecuted Jewish People for Centuries

On top of the fact that God has partially blinded the Jewish people, Christians have persecuted the Jewish people for centuries. This has contributed to many Jewish people not wanting to consider Christ.

That Christians persecuted Jewish people may disturb you. You may even say that they were likely *not* Christians if they persecuted Jewish people.

Well, they were Christians.

Regular, intense persecution of the Jewish people around the world and throughout the ages is astounding. A simple list to summarize their persecution

---

[2] "World Population," Worldometers, accessed May 26, 2017, www.worldometers.info.

is not possible. I was disheartened to find page after page listing dates with nations who historically either discriminated against, mocked, cursed, isolated, delegitimized, expelled, or murdered Jews. If you want to research this further, just Google "Jewish Persecution" to see a more comprehensive list.

Below is a *very* abbreviated list of persecutions done to the Jewish people, executed by people who acted in the name of Jesus Christ and Christianity:

Second Century

- Ignatius, bishop of Antioch, proclaimed in his Epistle to the Magnesians, that any form of Judaism is incompatible with belief in Jesus as Messiah.
- In Justin Martyr's "Dialogue with Trypho the Jew," he claims that the Jews had been replaced by the Church.
- Christians burned down a synagogue near the Euphrates River (in modern-day Syria).
- Jerome, the Latin Church Father, spoke out against the Jews and in the eyes of the Church, the Jews had become thoroughly demonized.
- Christian mobs destroyed synagogues in the cities of Antioch, Daphne, and Ravenna.
- Thousands of Jews were killed during civil unrest in Egypt, Cyprus, and Cyrenaica. Jews were expelled from Alexandria.

Fourth Century

- While Constantine's reign had some positive outcomes for Christians, he also enacted various discriminating laws regarding Jews, including a law that Jews could no longer live in Jerusalem.
- The Council of Nicea determined to forever separate the Christian celebration of Easter from its Jewish roots in the Passover, ignoring that Jesus and His disciples all celebrated Passover.
- Christian Emperor Constantius forbade marriage between Jewish men and Christian women—existing Christian/Jewish marriages were to be dissolved.

- Christian leader, John Chrysotom, claimed that because God hates the Jews, then Christians are "to hate them and long for their blood."[3]

Fifth Century

- Roman laws prohibited Jews from holding important positions involving money. They could not hold judicial or executive offices and were banned from building new synagogues.
- Severe persecutions began in Spain. Jews were given the option to convert to Christianity or be expelled. Many Jewish children over age six were taken from their parents to be reeducated as Christians.

Sixth Century

- The Byzantine Empire banned the use of the Hebrew language, and Jews were forbidden to worship. Jewish communities were converted by force, and their synagogues were turned into churches.

Seventh Century

- Spain ordered the burning of the Talmud and other "heretical" books.
- The king of Spain forced Jews to give all land, slaves, and buildings bought from Christians to his treasury and declared that all Jewish children over the age of seven be taken from their homes and raised as Christians.

Eleventh Century

- In Granada, Spain, Muslims crucified Jewish leaders and massacred over 4,000 in one day. Jews were forced to pay taxes to support the Catholic church.

---

[3] Ronald Diprose, *Israel and the Church: The Origins and Effects of replacement theology* (Waynesboro, GA: Authentic Media, 2004), 22.

- The First Crusade invaded Central European cities attacking the Jewish communities under the slogan, "Why fight Christ's enemies abroad when they are living among us?" Eight hundred Jews were killed and 1,200 committed suicide in Mainz, Germany, to escape being forced to convert to Christianity.
- The Crusaders forced all the Jews in Jerusalem into one synagogue and set it on fire. Those who escaped were forced back into the burning building.

Twelfth Century

- After a six-day siege, 500 Jews of York, England, were massacred by departing Crusaders.
- France imprisoned all Jews and demanded a ransom for release.
- Jews were considered to be enemies of the Christian religion. Jews were massacred in France in the cities of Carentan, Rameru, Sully, and Bohemia.
- King Philip Augustus seized all Jewish property and expelled the Jews from France. Synagogues were converted into churches.

Thirteenth Century

- Crusaders attacked Jewish communities in France and attempted to baptize all the Jews. The 3,000 who resisted were slaughtered. The Talmud was declared blasphemous in Paris—twenty-four cartloads of handwritten Talmudic manuscripts were burned. Public excoriations of Jews in the name of the Church became commonplace such as the Disputations of Paris. These "debates" pitted Jewish converts of the Church against the rabbinical community in a battle of the minds where messianic prophecy was debated. The king expelled Jews from France and confiscated their property and synagogues. Most moved to Germany.
- Vienna forced Jews to wear a cone-shaped headdress and yellow badges.

- London closed all synagogues and prohibited Jewish physicians from practicing on Christians. England passed the Statute of the Jewry, forcing Jews to wear an identifying yellow badge. Many Jews were arrested. The English hanged 300 Jews, whose property then went to the English crown. By 1290, King Edward I expelled all (16,000) Jews, leaving with only what they could carry. Many were robbed by authorities, and others drowned on their way to France. The Jews did not formally return to England until almost four hundred years later.

- German cathedral ceilings were decorated with obscene and dehumanizing imagery of Jews that remained for six hundred years. In Munich, Germany, a blood libel (a false incendiary claim against Jews, alleging that they murder Christians to use their blood for ritual purposes) resulted in deaths of 68 Jews; 180 more were burned alive in their synagogue.

Fourteenth Century

- One hundred thousand Jews were exiled from France, with only the clothes on their backs.

- After being blamed for the Black Death, Jews were murdered en masse in Germany. In Bavaria, 12,000 were massacred; in Erfurt, 3,000; in Tours, 160 were burned alive; in Strausberg, 2,000 were burned; in Mainz, 6,000 killed; and in Worms, 400 murdered.

- In Basel, Switzerland, 600 Jews were burned at the stake, 140 children were forcibly baptized, and the remaining Jews were expelled.

Fifteenth Century

- Jews were expelled from Austria and Geneva, Switzerland.

- During the Spanish Inquisition, King Ferdinand and Queen Isabella gave Jews the choice to either be baptized as Christians or be expelled from Spain—more than 100,000 were exiled.

- Spain and Portugal forced Jews to convert to Christianity. 10,000 Jews fled the country rather than be baptized as Christians.

Sixteenth Century

- Martin Luther, the great Protestant Reformer, attempted to convert Jews to Christianity. When his plan failed, he became enraged at the Jewish people and, towards the end of his life, wrote a book titled *The Jews and Their Lies,* dehumanizing and demonizing Jews. He advocated a plan to get rid of Jews. Many German towns expelled Jewish people, who were accused of ritual murder, black magic, and well poisoning.
- Pope Paul IV wrote, "It appears utterly absurd and impermissible that the Jews, whom God has condemned to eternal slavery for their guilt, should enjoy our Christian love." He renewed anti-Jewish legislation and installed locked ghettos in Rome.
- Russian Jews were given an ultimatum to embrace the Russian Orthodox Church or die—300 Jewish men, women and children were thrown into ice holes in a river.

Seventeenth Century

- Ukrainian Cossacks massacred about 100,000 Jews and many more were tortured.
- The *Pale of Settlement* took away many of the rights of the Jewish people in western Russia, including residency except for a limited number of Jews with university educations, members of affluent merchant guilds, particular artisans and some military personnel.

Eighteenth Century

- The Russian Orthodox Church intensified discriminatory policies toward the Jews.

Nineteenth Century

- Anti-Jewish riots in Germany spread to Denmark, Latvia, and Bohemia.
- The term "pogrom" became denotative of the violence against local Jewish populations.
- Moscow, Russia, the Russian Orthodox Church expelled 20,000 Jews.

Twentieth Century

- Masses of Jewish civilians (up to 250,000 estimated) were murdered and 300,000 were orphaned in pogroms in Odessa and during the Russian Civil War. Mobs were led by priests crying out to kill the Jews.
- The Leo Frank trial and lynching in Atlanta, Georgia, turned the spotlight on anti-Semitism in America and led to the expansion of the Ku Klux Klan.
- Increased anti-Semitism in the USA was led by the Ku Klux Klan, many whom identified themselves as Christians.
- Nuremburg laws in Germany defined the Jewish race and stripped Jews of citizenship, the right to work and of their rights as human beings.
- On *Kristallnacht* (the night of broken glass), most German synagogues and hundreds of Jewish-owned German businesses were destroyed. One hundred Jews were killed and 10,000 were sent to concentration camps.
- The United States, who often identified itself as a Christian country, refused to accept Jews who tried to escape Nazi Germany. (Thirty other countries also refused to help the Jews).
- In 1939, the "Voyage of the Damned," the ocean liner *St. Louis*, carrying 907 Jewish refugees from Germany, was turned back by the USA just as the refugees were in view of the coast.
- The U.S. Congress rejected efforts to accept 20,000 Jewish refugee children under the age of fourteen from Nazi, Germany.

- During the Holocaust about 6.5 million Jews, including 1.5 million children, were systematically killed by Nazi Germany. Hitler identified himself as a Christian.

Twenty-First Century

- Iranian president Mahmoud Ahmadinejad widened hostility between Iran and Israel by denying the Holocaust and calling for Jewish genocide.
- During 2007–2008, Jewish communities around the world were rocked by fire bombings, assaults, and death threats during the Gaza War.
- During 2014's Operation Protective Edge, Hamas kidnapped three Israeli Jewish teenagers, triggering a seven-week war, which Israel is blamed for starting.

This list is sobering—and there were many other anti-Semitic incidents in history. We need to understand and appreciate what the Jewish people have endured. Jewish children are educated about these historic persecutions and are understandably wary of Christians.

Some challenge me and say that those murdering the Jewish people were really not Christians. I ask if they believe Martin Luther was a Christian. He did a lot of damage to the Jewish people. Hitler used Luther's writings as justification for annihilating the Jewish people.

Even if some of those calling themselves Christians were not actually Christians, is it really the responsibility of the Jewish person to determine who was and who was not a true Christian? When you see the consistent opposition to the Jewish people, you may gain a better understanding of why Jewish people do not trust Christians. It may also help you understand why they have such difficulty accepting Jesus Christ as Messiah.

Perhaps some Jewish people are waiting for Christians to apologize for the wrongs committed against them by our forefathers. We might consider humbling ourselves enough to ask our Jewish friends to forgive *us*. Some challenge me and say that those murdering the Jewish people were really not Christians.

I attended a meeting years ago in a home where many who were pro-Israel were invited. The homeowner invited one of her friends who was Jewish. She sat quietly in the back and listened.

When the speaker was made aware that there was a Jewish woman in the group, he stopped his presentation and began speaking to her directly as if she were the only one in the room. He told her that he was ashamed that his Christian forefathers were involved in persecuting Jewish people and asked her if she would accept his apology on their behalf. As he spoke lovingly to her and with all sincerity, her eyes welled up with tears.

She didn't speak, but nodded her head in recognition of what had happened in the past and that this stranger calling himself a Christian was asking her forgiveness.

Perhaps Jewish people do not know that some of us would give our lives for them. Perhaps they do not know that we also are angry about their history of persecution. Would it be so difficult if we humbled ourselves and offered our apologies to our Jewish friends and let them know that we stand with them?

Why have the Jews been persecuted for centuries? Many Christians have accused the Jews of being Christ-killers. They even hold this current generation responsible. Did the Jews kill Jesus? Some certainly were responsible. Romans were also responsible. *We* are responsible because of our sin. However, before the beginning of time Jesus planned to willingly give up His life. Jesus says in John 10:17–18, "Therefore My Father loves Me, because I lay down My life that I may take it again. No one takes it from Me, but I lay it down of Myself. I have power to lay it down, and I have power to take it again. This command I have received from My Father." So, out of love for His Father, Jesus *willingly* gave His life. Ephesians 1:4 confirms that "He chose us in Him before the foundation of the world."

Reason 3: Much of Christianity is Void of its Jewish Roots

To the Jewish person, Jesus is the Christian god, separate from the God of Abraham. Many Jews do not know who Jesus Christ is. They think Jesus is just the son of Mr. and Mrs. Christ. The Jewish people do not realize that Jesus came as *their* Messiah, as prophesied in their Scriptures. They do not realize that the Christian biblical roots are the same as theirs. One reason is that many of our biblical roots have disappeared from our teachings in church. Not only has this made it difficult for Jewish persons to relate to Christianity, but it has also robbed Gentile believers of an understanding of our rich heritage!

To show you how far things have gone, it is estimated that more than 75 percent of American churches believe the lie that Gentile Christians (the Church) have replaced Israel in God's promises. This will be discussed further in chapter 9.

Much of what Christians practice today is not recognizable to the Jewish person because Christianity's Jewish roots are not emphasized.

For example, God commanded that the day of worship, the Sabbath, be Friday night through Saturday night, and the Jewish people still observe this. However, this was changed in Christianity to Sunday when the Catholic church officially changed the day of worship from Saturday to Sunday after the edict by Constantine the Great in AD 321.

Christians also do not recognize the Jewish appointed days (referred to as the Jewish feasts) within the Christian church. Most believers do not know the significance of these holidays and are therefore missing a beautiful part of their heritage and how these holy days teach us a deeper understanding of the holiness of God. We must realize that this makes it even more difficult for a Jewish person to step into Christianity, which looks very different from what they read in Scripture!

Furthermore, Scripture teaches in Romans 11:17 that as believers, we are grafted into their roots—they are not grafted into ours.

Persecution of the Jewish people will not end until the Prince of Peace comes to rule and reign. You can see why it is so difficult to share the gospel with the Jewish people. They have been persecuted and killed throughout history—so many times "in the name of Jesus" that they see Christians as enemies.

CHAPTER 3

Four Covenants Woven Together

A covenant is like a contract—legal and binding on both parties for its fulfillment. It is an agreement made by one person to another person, to a specific group of people, or to humanity in general. It can be conditional or unconditional and it can be one-sided or two-sided.

To know if it is conditional or unconditional, one would look for words like *if* and *then*. If either party fails to meet its responsibilities, then the covenant is broken and neither party must fulfill the expectations of the covenant.

Unconditional covenants do not require anything on the part of the receiving person or group. A one-sided covenant puts the burden of responsibility on one person only, whereas a two-sided covenant contains a shared agreement of responsibility. For example, marriage is a two-sided covenant in which a man and a woman legally commit to love and honor one another and be legally tied together for a lifetime. An example of a one-sided contract would be a financial loan where the burden to repay is on one side only.

God has made many different types of covenants with mankind. Although there are many more than what we will delve into, we will look at the four major covenants and discover how they are interwoven.

Abrahamic Covenant

God made a covenant with Abram and his descendants. It began with a call on Abram, which is found in Genesis 12:1–3.

> Now the Lord had said to Abram: "Get out of your country, from your family and from your father's house, to a land that I will show you. I will make you a great nation; I will bless you and make your name great; and you shall be a blessing. I will bless those who bless you, and I will curse him who curses you; and in you all the families of the earth shall be blessed."

Abram obeyed God, left his home with his family and was directed to go to the land of Canaan, where God said He would give him and his descendants (in Hebrew, seed) that land (Genesis 12:7).

God affirmed His covenant to Abram in Genesis 13:14–16.

> "Lift your eyes now and look from the place where you are—northward, southward, eastward, and westward; for all the land which you see I give to you and your descendants forever. And I will make your descendants as the dust of the earth; so that if a man could number the dust of the earth, then your descendants also could be numbered."

But Abram questioned God's covenant. Abram was seventy-five years of age when he and his family departed Haran. It was likely several years later when Abram had a visit from God, shared his concern that he had no offspring, and questioned God's promise to him (Genesis 15:1–3). God once again affirmed that Abram would have many descendants.

Abram asked how he would know that he would inherit this land, and God took him outside to look toward heaven and count the stars. God said if Abram could count the stars, he would know how many descendants he would have, and Abram believed God. Then God "cut" (confirmed) the covenant (Genesis 15).

In the days of Abram, when two parties wanted to enter into a formal agreement, animals would be used as part of the ceremony. The parties would gather a number of specific animals, kill them, and arrange their carcasses on the ground so that half of the carcass was on one side and half on the other with enough space between each half to create a path through which both parties to the contract would pass together as they swore to uphold their end of the covenant. If they did not live up to their part of the covenant, they could receive the fate of these animals. This is often called "cutting covenant." The covenant process was very serious. It was legally binding, just as a signed contract would be today.

The covenant is confirmed (signed) in Genesis 15.

> So He [God] said to him [Abram], "Bring Me a three-year-old heifer, a three-year-old female goat, a three-year-old ram, a turtledove, and a young pigeon." Then he brought all these to Him and cut them in two, down the middle, and placed each piece opposite the other; but he did not cut the birds in two. And when the vultures came down on the carcasses, Abram drove them away. Now when the sun was going down, a deep sleep fell upon Abram; and behold, horror and great darkness fell on him. (vss. 9–12)

> And it came to pass, when the sun went down and it was dark, that behold, there was a smoking oven and a burning torch that passed between those pieces. On the same day the LORD made a covenant with Abram, saying: "To your descendants I have given this land, from the river of Egypt to the great river, the River Euphrates." (vss. 17–18)

God's covenant with Abram is unconditional. From these scriptures, we can see that this covenant is one-sided and unconditional. Abram was put into a deep sleep, so he could not pass between the carcass pieces as God did. Therefore, Abram did not "sign the contract," as one might expect. Rather, it is unconditional because God did not ask Abram to do anything—the burden of responsibility is completely on God's shoulders. For Abram, it was "no strings attached."

Pottery	Symbolism	Use
Smoking oven or fire pot	God Almighty—the Eternal Flame	Sealed container kept coals hot all night
Lamp with four wicks (torches)	Jesus as the Light of the World	Lamp held four wicks (torches)
Olive Oil	Holy Spirit	Olive oil is the fuel that kept the torches burning

God spells out the terms of the covenant in Genesis 17:2–11.

> "And I will make My covenant between Me and you, and will multiply you exceedingly." Then Abram fell on his face and God talked with him, saying: "As for me, behold, My covenant is with you, and you shall be a father of many nations. No longer shall your name be called Abram, but your name shall be Abraham; for I have made you a father of many nations. I will make you exceedingly fruitful; and I will make nations of you, and kings shall come from you. And I will establish My covenant between me and you and your descendants after you in their generations, for an everlasting covenant, to be God to you and your descendants after you. Also I give to you and your descendants after you the land in which you are a stranger, all the land of Canaan, as an everlasting possession; and I will be their God."

> And God said to Abraham: "As for you, you shall keep My covenant, you and your descendants after you throughout their generations. This is My covenant which you shall keep, between Me and you and your descendants after you: Every male child among you shall be circumcised; and you

shall be circumcised in the flesh of your foreskins, and it shall be a sign of the covenant between Me and you."

One very important thing to note is that God has stated His covenant is "everlasting." This very important covenant has four main components:

- The promise of **land** as an everlasting possession (Genesis 17:2–8)
- The promise of **descendants** (seed) (Genesis 12:2, 13:14–16)
- The promise of **blessing** (Genesis 12:2–3)
- The sign of **circumcision** (Genesis 17:11)

It is important to note that this covenant is established with Abraham's younger son Isaac as the sole inheritor. This is significant, especially in today's modern world, because Islam claims the covenant was made through Abraham's older son Ishmael. God told Abraham that the son of promise would come from Abraham and his wife, Sarah.

> Then God said: "No, Sarah your wife shall bear you a son, and you shall call his name Isaac; I will establish My covenant with him for an everlasting covenant, and with his descendants after him. And as for Ishmael, I have heard you. Behold, I have blessed him, and will make him fruitful, and will multiply him exceedingly. He shall beget twelve princes, and I will make him a great nation. But My covenant I will establish with Isaac, whom Sarah shall bear to you at this set time next year." (Genesis 17:19–21)

Ishmael was the offspring of Sarah's Egyptian handmaiden, Hagar. He received a different blessing in verse 20. Note that twice God says his covenant is established with Isaac—not Ishmael. God later reaffirmed this covenant through Isaac in Genesis 26:3–5.

Because Abraham believed God, it was accounted to him for righteousness (Genesis 15:6). The gospel was given to Abraham; those who are of faith are sons of Abraham.

And the Scripture, foreseeing that God would justify the nations [Gentiles] by faith, preached the gospel to Abraham beforehand, saying, "In you all the nations shall be blessed." So then those who are of faith are blessed with believing Abraham. (Galatians 3:8–9)

A torch holder (left) and smoking oven, as referenced in Genesis 15:17. Photo by Thomas Winder.

Archaeologist Thomas Winder, formerly with Trinity Southwest University in Albuquerque, New Mexico, explains how God's plan of redemption can be found in ancient pottery. He uses these artifacts to explain that God had to come Himself to pay the cost for humanity and put the responsibility of keeping covenant on His shoulders alone.

The smoking oven (fire pot) symbolizes God Almighty ... the Eternal Flame. It was used in ancient times to keep coals warm all night and ready for use in the morning. The lamp with four wicks (torches) symbolizes Jesus as the Light of the World. The wicks (torches) were placed on all four corners of their holder, that is, in the cardinal directions of north, south, east, and west. They were fueled by olive oil, which symbolizes the Holy Spirit. Thus

Father, Son, and Holy Spirit passed between the pieces of meat to make covenant with Abraham.

The New Testament refers to the Abrahamic Covenant many times. A few examples are Romans 4:11–13; Galatians 3:8, 3:29; and Hebrews 6:13–15.

The three major components of the Abrahamic Covenant are spelled out in detail in *other* covenants:

- The Land—Title Deed covenant (Deuteronomy 30:1–10)
- The Seed (Descendants)—The Davidic Covenant (2 Samuel 7:11b-16; 1 Chronicles 17:10b-14, Psalm 89:36; Jeremiah 33:17)
- The Blessing—The new covenant (Jeremiah 31:31–34; Matthew 5:17, 26:28; Luke 22:20; Romans 8:2–6; 1 Corinthians 5:3–4, 11:25; Galatians 3:19; Hebrews 9:15–17)

With most of the covenants God made with man, God attached a sign. The sign of the Abrahamic Covenant is circumcision. Every male descendant was required to be circumcised (Genesis 17:10–14).

Mosaic Covenant

It is never to be assumed that a new covenant replaces another or makes a preceding covenant void. When God gives a new covenant, He will explain whether it is to replace an old one or is to be added to a previous covenant and whether it is conditional or unconditional. The Abrahamic Covenant was never annulled, replaced, or retracted, but the Law was added to this covenant because of man's sin.

The Mosaic Covenant was added to the Abrahamic Covenant. Galatians 3:19 confirms this: "What purpose then does the Law [Mosaic Covenant] serve? It was added because of transgressions, till the Seed should come to whom the promise was made." This verse gives us the purpose for it.

The Law referred to is the Mosaic Covenant or Law of Moses. The people of Israel were sinning and needed a code of laws and practices to guide their behavior as well as separate them from the surrounding nations and cultures. Where there is sin, there is chaos. But God is a God of order. So the Mosaic Law was given. It reveals to the people of Israel, and indeed, all humanity, their sinfulness and their need for a Savior. The Law points to a future Seed, the Promise, and indicates that the Law would be fulfilled in this Seed, which is Jesus.

The Mosaic Covenant is based on the shedding of innocent blood for the atonement of sins: "For the life of the flesh is in the blood, and I have given it to you upon the altar to make atonement for your souls; for it is the blood that makes atonement for the soul" (Leviticus 17:11). With the Mosaic Covenant, there was only temporary propitiation for sin. The High Priest would have to make atonement each year for the sins of the people.

Everything in the Mosaic law pointed to the cross.

Does this mean that by keeping the Law one could be saved? No, the Law never saved, but became a tutor to point mankind to the Messiah—the Savior. With the Law came sacrifices to cover sin but it could only *cover* sin—not satisfy the penalty for it. "Therefore the Law was our tutor to bring us to Christ [Messiah], that we might be justified by faith" (Galatians 3:24). It was given to Israel to govern her life in the Promised Land *and* to show mankind his total helpless and hopeless condition before a righteous and just God—to point man to the need for salvation.

Salvation can only come through faith (Habakkuk 2:4). We have shown that Abraham had faith in God and it was accounted to him for righteousness. Salvation has always been by faith alone. Christ promises that it is this very law that He came to fulfill (Matthew 5:17). He became the final blood sacrifice—no more animals were necessary—all the sacrifices were fulfilled in Christ.

The Mosaic Covenant was an agreement made between God and the children of Israel alone, through Moses. It required obedience to 613 commandments found throughout the books of the Law for Israel to be blessed:

> If you diligently heed the voice of the LORD your God and do what is right in His sight, give ear to His commandments and keep all His statutes, I will put none of the diseases on you which I have brought on the Egyptians. For I am the LORD who heals you. (Exodus 15:26)

The requirement of the Israelites' obedience makes the Mosaic Covenant a conditional covenant, based on obedience. This is different from the Abrahamic Covenant in which God made all the promises and did not require anything of Abraham. God promised blessings to the Israelites for their obedience to the Laws, but if they disobeyed them, God promised punishment. The specific blessings and curses related to the Mosaic Covenant are found in Deuteronomy 28.

After God established the unconditional covenant with Abraham, we see that Israel was a chosen nation—a vehicle used by God to bless all the nations. God was to rule and guide this nation in her destiny so she might not become polluted or contaminated by the other nations and their gods, so Israel might fulfill her purpose.

The Mosaic Law was given to direct Israel as a nation in all areas of life—moral, social, religious, political, and economic. The Law was designed to set Israel apart from the nations. The Law is seen as holy and good, according to Paul, and it is a means to separate Israel from the sins of the godless nations. These laws, also often referred to as the Laws of Moses, can be found in Exodus 19–24 and throughout the book of Leviticus. It was a temporary covenant that later would be fulfilled by the Messiah's sacrifice in the New Covenant.

The Abrahamic Covenant was not replaced and, therefore, continues today and forever. The Mosaic Covenant has been fulfilled (not replaced) by the New Covenant.

In the Hebrew Scriptures, the word *Law* is *Torah*, which translates as *instruction*. The definition of *law* is a system of principles or rules that instructs man as to God's will and direction.

The New Testament refers to the Mosaic Covenant many times because it is clear that the New Covenant fulfills it. But that does not mean the Law is not useful. Paul tells us in 2 Timothy 3:16–17 that "All Scripture is given by inspiration of God, and is profitable for doctrine, for reproof, for correction, for instruction in righteousness, that the man of God may be complete, thoroughly equipped for every good work."

Another example is Hebrews 8:6–9.

> But now He has obtained a more excellent ministry, inasmuch as He is also Mediator of a better covenant, which was established on better promises. For if that first covenant had been faultless, then no place would have been sought for a second. Because finding fault with them, He says: "Behold, the days are coming, says the LORD, when I will make a New Covenant with the house of Israel and with the house of Judah—not according to the covenant I made with their fathers in the day when I took them by the hand to lead them out of the land of Egypt; because they did not continue in My covenant, and I disregarded them, says the LORD."

The sign of the Mosaic Covenant is the two tablets of stone.

New Covenant

The Mosaic Covenant which God established with His people required obedience to the Old Testament Mosaic Law. Because the wages of sin is death, according to Romans 6:23, the Law required that people perform rituals and sacrifices in order to please God and remain in His grace.

However, Scripture points out in Jeremiah 31:32 that the Mosaic Covenant was broken by Israel, even though God kept His promises and foretold that there would be a time when He would make a New Covenant with the nation of Israel. Verse 32 says, "not according to the covenant that

I made with their fathers in the day that I took them by the hand to bring them out of the land of Egypt, My covenant which they broke, though I was a husband to them,' says the LORD." Israel continuously disobeyed God.

Jeremiah 31:31 gives us the description of the New Covenant: "Behold, the days are coming, says the LORD, when I will make a New Covenant with the house of Israel and with the house of Judah." From this verse we know that the New Covenant would be made with Israel and Judah. At the time of Jeremiah, it was yet in the future. Although the Old Testament references to the New Covenant were for the nation of Israel, those who put their faith in Jesus the Messiah also share in its provisions. Like the Abrahamic Covenant, which was ratified with Abraham and his national seed and yet contained blessing for Gentiles, so the New Covenant can also be applied to the Gentiles.

Verse 33 continues, "But this is the covenant that I will make with the house of Israel after those days, says the LORD: I will put My law in their minds, and write it on their hearts; and I will be their God, and they shall be My people." God reaffirms that this covenant is with Israel. Obviously, God has not yet put His Law in the minds of the Jewish people and has not written it on their hearts. As a nation, Israel has not yet found Messiah. Because these things have not yet occurred, we can again conclude that these things will be fulfilled in the future.

Physical Promises

The New Covenant has physical promises for Israel (such as restored land, physical blessings, freedom from oppression, and forgiveness of sin). We can see Israel being restored today, but it is only a precursor to what will be in full. Before this covenant can be put into effect, there must be a national salvation and restoration of all Israel, as spoken of in Romans 11.

> And so all Israel will be saved, as it is written: "The Deliverer will come out of Zion, and he will turn away ungodliness from Jacob; for this is My covenant with them, when I take away their sins." (Romans 11:26–27)

We can look forward to the day when "all Israel will be saved" (Romans 11:26) and the land of Israel will be inhabited in full.

In Jeremiah 31:34 we read, "No more shall every man teach his neighbor, and every man his brother, saying, 'Know the LORD,' for they all shall know Me, from the least of them to the greatest of them, says the LORD. For I will forgive their iniquity, and their sin I will remember no more."

The Old Testament Anticipated a New Covenant

Hebrews 8:8–12 quotes the New Covenant with *Israel* to show that the Old Testament anticipated a New Covenant. The old covenant required that a priest make animal sacrifices on behalf of the sin of the people and of himself. In the New Covenant, Jesus Christ became the final blood sacrifice for all sins...once for all. This puts us under grace, and no other blood sacrifices are required. This is a better covenant.

Salvation Under a New Covenant

Galatians 3:19 tells us that the Law was in effect *until* the Seed should come. The Messiah was that Seed, and with the New Covenant He released mankind from the penalty of the Law. Repeatedly, the New Testament clearly states that Christians are dead to the effects of the Mosaic Law, meaning that the Law cannot condemn us because we are under grace (Romans 6:14, 7:1–14; 2 Corinthians 3:7–18; Galatians 3:10–14, 24–25, 5:1, 13). However, it is God's desire that we live righteously as His Law is now written on our hearts, and our obedience pleases Him (Romans 6:1–2, 3:31, 7:12; 1 John 3:22). We are under grace.

If we have found salvation in Jesus, we are under the New Covenant; we are no longer under the penalty of the Law. Everyone, Jew and Gentile, is given the opportunity to receive the free gift of salvation (Ephesians 2:8–9). Hebrews 9:15–17 explains about our eternal inheritance:

> And for this reason He is the Mediator of the New Covenant, by means of death, for the redemption of the

transgressions under the first covenant, that those who are called may receive the promise of the eternal inheritance. For where there is a testament, there must also of necessity be the death of the testator. For a testament is in force after men are dead, since it has no power at all while the testator lives.

These verses explain that with the death of Christ, the New Covenant is in force. He is the Mediator of a better covenant, which was established upon better promises (Hebrews 8:6). God refers to the New Covenant as being better because when God established the New Covenant, He guaranteed that Israel would be successful living in obedience to it because of grace.

Salvation is for anyone who has faith in Messiah Jesus, who provides forgiveness of sin, eternal life, the indwelling of the Holy Spirit, and daily communion with our Father.

Jesus' death on the cross paid the price of salvation for the Jew and the Gentile. Jewish people may individually find salvation now, just as the Gentiles who come to Him now—by faith in Jesus.

> For the law of the Spirit of life in Christ Jesus has made me free from the law of sin and death. For what the law could not do in that it was weak through the flesh, God did by sending His own Son in the likeness of sinful flesh, on account of sin: He condemned sin in the flesh, that the righteous requirement of the Law might be fulfilled in us who do not walk according to the flesh but according to the Spirit. (Romans 8:2–5).

Jesus referenced the New Covenant during the Last Supper (the Last Passover) and linked His death with the New Covenant. The disciples understood that He was referring to the New Covenant referenced in Jeremiah 31. Jesus says in Matthew 26:28, "For this is My blood of the New Covenant, which is shed for many for the remission of sins" (See also Luke 22:20 and 1 Corinthians 11:25).

Because we are no longer under the penalty of the Law, does this mean that we can sin all we want? As Romans 6:1–2 says, certainly not!

Matthew 5:17 tells us that Jesus Christ came to fulfill the Law of Moses but not destroy it. Jesus did not come to abolish the Law but to make full the meaning of what the Torah and the ethical demands of the Prophets required. Thus He came to complete our understanding of the Torah and the Prophets, so we can try more effectively to be and do what they say to be and do.

The New Covenant is unconditional, completes the Mosaic Covenant, and recognizes different applications for Israel and the Church. The church is never called *Israel* in the New Testament, and we should not try to spiritualize Scripture to fit into our point of view. The church can never fulfill any of the covenants that God has made specifically with Israel.

The Church and the New Covenant

The question often raised is "How does the Church relate to the New Covenant?"

Foundationally, all covenants were given to Israel, but believers are grafted into salvation and into the covenants as well. This is explained in Ephesians 2:11–14:

> Therefore remember that you, once Gentiles in the flesh—
> who are called Uncircumcision by what is called the
> Circumcision made in the flesh by hands—that at that time
> you were without Christ, being aliens from the common-
> wealth of Israel and strangers from the covenants of prom-
> ise, having no hope and without God in the world. But now
> in Christ Jesus you who once were far off have been made
> near by the blood of Christ. For He Himself is our peace,
> who has made both one, and has broken down the middle
> wall of division between us.

Is God's Promise to the Jewish Nation in Effect Today?

Jeremiah 31:35–36 explains that God's promise to the Jewish nation will last as long as there is a sun, moon, stars, earth, and sea. This is an unconditional promise. No one can change it no matter what they do.

> Thus says the LORD, who gives the sun for a light by day, the ordinances of the moon and stars for a light by night, who disturbs the sea, and its waves roar (the LORD of hosts is His name): "If those ordinances depart from before Me, says the LORD, Then the seed of Israel shall also cease from being a nation before Me forever."

The Legal Contract Signed

How was this contract signed (ratified)? In the same manner that the old covenant was confirmed—by the shedding of blood. However, instead of the shed blood of an animal for each and every sin, Jesus Christ provided the blood sacrifice—once for all. No further blood sacrifices would be required (Hebrews 10:10).

Davidic Covenant

This covenant was made between God and David and promised two things: (1) an eternal occupancy of David's throne and (2) that the kingdom would be everlasting (2 Samuel 7:16). In addition, God promised that David's seed would endure forever (Psalm 89:36–37). In Jeremiah 33:17 God promised "David shall never lack a man to sit on the throne of the house of Israel."

The covenant is summarized in 1 Chronicles 17:11–14 when Nathan the prophet spoke to David with words from God:

> "And it shall be, when your days are fulfilled, when you must go to be with your fathers, that I will set up your seed after you, who will be of your sons; and I will establish his

kingdom. He shall build Me a house, and I will establish his throne forever. I will be his Father, and he shall be My son; and I will not take My mercy away from him, as I took it from him who was before you. And I will establish him in My house and in My kingdom forever, and his throne shall be established forever."

Similarly, the angel Gabriel promised that Jesus Christ would reign over the house of Jacob forever (Luke 1:19, 26–33). The Jewish people understood this from the 1 Chronicles 17 passage. Jesus confirmed this message when He taught that the kingdom was at hand. After His resurrection, Jesus gave more information about this covenant, telling the disciples that the timing of the restoration is not for them to know (Acts 1:6–7).

The Abrahamic Covenant promises a seed (descendants) and the Davidic Covenant confirms that but additionally promises a throne and a kingdom that will last forever (2 Samuel 7:13).

The Davidic Covenant is an unconditional and everlasting covenant. However, because Israel was not a nation for two thousand years (between AD 70 and 1948), the throne awaited occupancy. Interruptions in the reign were temporary. This covenant points to a future fulfillment. Revelation 20–21 gives us the details. Revelation 20:4 shows us Christ reigning for a thousand years. After the thousand years, Revelation 21 gives us a picture of the new heaven, the new earth, and the New Jerusalem established on earth.

The future throne will be here on earth during the thousand-year reign of Christ. Jesus Christ is the one who fulfills the Davidic Covenant on earth during that time.

Some have spiritualized this promise and say we are now living in the thousand years and the Church is reigning (the Church Age). However, this kingdom should be expected literally. The Jewish people throughout biblical history expected a literal kingdom. Jesus and the disciples explained a literal kingdom.

We can look forward with assurance and expectancy that the thousand year kingdom will come and Jesus Christ will rule and reign over the house of David!

Summary

There is a progression through the four covenants mentioned in this chapter.

God first established His covenant with the Hebrew (Jewish) people through Abraham, Isaac and Jacob in the **Abrahamic Covenant.**

Then, because of the sinfulness of the people, God added the **Mosaic Covenant** to cover their sin through the blood sacrifice of animals, pointing them to the Messiah. The Mosaic Covenant was broken, not by God but by the people.

A **New Covenant** was promised to the house of Judah and to the house of Israel, ensuring they would know God. This covenant will write God's law in their minds and on their hearts—and they will know God. The New Covenant provides a way of salvation to all those who trust Messiah, He who became the final blood sacrifice for sin.

The **Davidic Covenant** adds to the Abrahamic Covenant, promising that the seed mentioned in the Abrahamic Covenant would produce a ruler who would reign forever. That ruler was prophesied as being the promised Messiah, Yeshua, Jesus the Christ.

For more detail about these covenants, see "Covenant Chart" in the Appendix.

Yeshua is the key to the fulfillment of all of God's covenants. He is the offspring of Abraham; He is the Davidic King; He is the final sacrifice, sealing the New Covenant with His blood. We can see God's eternal plan for Israel woven throughout these four precious covenants.

Covenant	Conditional	Unconditional	One-sided	Two-sided	Temporary	Permanent
Abrahamic		x	x			x
Mosaic	x			x	x	
New		x		x		x
Davidic		x	x			x

CHAPTER 4

The Relationship between Jews and Gentiles

Over the centuries, the Church has strayed from what the Scriptures teach us about the proper relationship between Jews and Gentiles. As Gentiles, we have clear teaching about our role with the Jewish people today.

First, let's understand the definition of *Gentile*. A Gentile is anyone *other* than a Jewish person. A Gentile can become Jewish by adopting the faith and lifestyle of a Jew, but a Jewish person can never become a Gentile. A good example of a Gentile person becoming Jewish is Ruth, a Moabitess. In Ruth 1:16 she says, " … wherever you go, I will go; and wherever you lodge, I will lodge; your people shall be my people, and your God, my God." Later, Ruth marries Boaz, and from their descendants comes King David.

The Jewish people are children of Abraham through natural lineage from Abraham, Isaac, and Jacob; some of these people simultaneously share in a spiritual lineage because they have faithfully kept God's Law. Believers in Jesus Christ are children of Abraham through a spiritual lineage. God's purpose in this spiritual lineage is separate from his purpose and work with the nation of Israel. [4]

---

[4] Timothy P. Jones, David Gundersen, and Benjamin Galan, *Rose Guide to End-Times Prophecy*, (Torrance, Calif., Rose Publishing, Inc., 2011), 58

For a Gentile believer, one of the most precious portions of Scripture is that of being grafted into the Jewish roots by way of salvation. This can be found in Romans 11:11–24, where Paul teaches about the olive tree. But first, some background.

Olive Trees and Olive Oil

Historically, the olive tree was very important to Israel's economy. Not only were olives used for food, but olive oil provided fuel for their lamps; it was their only lubricating oil; it was a preserving agent; it was used as a healing salve. The way we use petroleum today is the way they used olive oil then. Crushing olives for oil in Israel was a leading industry—comparable to our own Kraft Foods or Johnson & Johnson in America today.

During the time of Jesus, new olive-pressing technologies were being used. In one system, the olives were collected from the gnarly-looking trees. To process the fruit, the workers would place the harvested olives in a large circular stone basin which held a huge wheel-shaped millstone. The mill-stone had a hole in the middle of it into which a thick wooden pole would be inserted. Attached to a donkey or a laborer, the millstone would then be moved around the basin, cracking the olives as it rolled over them.

A millstone in Capernaum, Israel. Photo by Deby Brown.

Next, the cracked olives would be put into something like a burlap bag and placed under a stone column which rested on a stone base. This column would be four or five feet tall, about twelve inches square and of enormous weight. This olive press was called a *gethsemane*. This pressing process was sometimes done in a cave so the column could be suspended from a huge crossbeam. With this tremendous weight on the cracked olives, it wasn't long before the precious oil would flow out from under the bottom of the column and drain into waiting jars or storage containers.

The *gethsemane* that squeezed or pressed the oil from the olives was very familiar to Jesus. *Gethsemanes* were just part of the landscape in those days.

Jesus spent the last few hours before His arrest in an olive garden (John 18:1) at a place called Gethsemane (Matthew 26:36). It is likely that this was somewhere on the Mount of Olives (Luke 22:39) where the olives of the nearby groves were pressed. He came there to pray.

A gethsemane in Capernaum, Israel. Photo by Deby Brown.

In that garden of Gethsemane, that garden of oil presses, Jesus got on His knees and experienced the weight that would be on Him at the cross—and the weight was so heavy that it squeezed out of Him His own blood. The weight caused Him to sweat drops of blood (Luke 22:44). He was heavily pressed as He knew He would carry the sin of the entire world, but He also knew that by doing this, He would bring about forgiveness of sins.

Did Jesus go to the garden of Gethsemene to illustrate that, symbolically, the olives are Jesus and that the weight of the gethsemane is you and me? I believe *we* are the gethsemane in this story. We are the reason His sweat turned to blood and the reason He went to that cross and took our sins and carried them. *You* became Jesus's gethsemane. The image of the great weight of a gethsemane on the precious olives can help us imagine the pressure Jesus felt as He contemplated the burden He was to bear—the cross. His blood became the symbol for the anointing He provides for those who love Him.

In John 14:6, Jesus says, "I am the way, the truth and the life. No one comes to the Father, but through Me." He is talking about that cross. No one can be made right before God—no one can make it to heaven—except through Jesus and the price He paid for our sins on that cross.

Read the actual prayer that Jesus prayed to His Father in this garden, found in John 17. You will not want to miss this—it is such a blessing to be able to read the *very* prayer Jesus prayed for you!

The Jewish Rejection of Messiah Allows Gentiles to be Grafted into the Promise

With that background about the olive tree, we can now look at Romans 11:11–24, where Paul explained how the Jews' rejection of Jesus as Messiah opens the door for Gentiles to be grafted into the faith.

> I say then, have they [the Jews] stumbled that they should fall? Certainly not! But through their fall, to provoke them to jealousy, salvation has come to the Gentiles. Now if their fall is riches for the world, and their failure riches for the Gentiles, how much more their fullness! For I speak to you Gentiles; inasmuch as I am an apostle to the Gentiles, I magnify my ministry, if by any means I may provoke to

jealousy those who are my flesh and save some of them. For if their being cast away is the reconciling of the world, what will their acceptance be but life from the dead? For if the first fruit is holy, the lump is also holy; and if the root is holy, so are the branches. And if some of the branches were broken off, and you, being a wild olive tree, were grafted in among them, and with them became a partaker of the root and fatness of the olive tree, do not boast against the branches. But if you boast, remember that you do not support the root, but the root supports you. You will say then, "Branches were broken off that I might be grafted in." Well said. Because of unbelief they were broken off, and you stand by faith. Do not be haughty, but fear. For if God did not spare the natural branches, he may not spare you either. Therefore, consider the goodness and severity of God: on those who fell, severity; but toward you, goodness, if you continue in His goodness. Otherwise you also will be cut off. And they also, if they do not continue in unbelief, will be grafted in, for God is able to graft them in again. For if you were cut out of the olive tree which is wild by nature, and were grafted contrary to nature into a cultivated olive tree, how much more will these, who are the natural branches, be grafted into their own olive tree?

You are only a part of this olive tree if you are a believer in Jesus Christ, regardless of whether you are Jewish or Gentile. The roots of this tree are the roots of the Jewish faith with such patriarchs as Abraham, Isaac, Jacob, Moses, and David. They believed in the shadow of the cross and were saved by faith. For example, Abraham "... believed in the LORD, and He accounted it to him for righteousness" (Genesis 15:6, Romans 4:3, Galatians 3:8). These patriarchs give the tree support. Gentiles are grafted into a tree of Jewish belief and are supported by the roots.

Olive trees have been known to live for more than two thousand years. Sometimes they stop bearing olives and, to promote growth, a wild olive branch is grafted into the main tree. Once the grafting takes place, not only does the new shoot bear fruit, but the original tree begins bearing fruit once again. This practice was illustrated symbolically by Paul in Romans 11.

The broken off branches are those who are Jewish, originally part of the tree, but broken off because of their lack of belief in Jesus, the Messiah. They are all welcome to be grafted back into this tree, once they trust in Him as Messiah. The wild olive branches are the Gentiles that are grafted into the tree when they also trust in the person of Jesus as their Messiah. Therefore, everyone in the tree trusts in Him.

Because we are grafted into the olive tree, we are considered adopted as sons by Jesus Christ Himself (Ephesians 1:5) into God's family and we are also heirs (Romans 8:17). Ephesians 2:11–13, and 19 remind us what our fate would have been without grafting:

> Therefore, remember that you, once Gentiles in the flesh—who are called Uncircumcision by what is called the Circumcision made in the flesh by hands—that at that time you were without Christ, being aliens from the commonwealth of Israel and strangers from the covenants of promise, having no hope and without God in the world. But now in Christ Jesus you who once were far off have been made near by the blood of Christ.… Now, therefore, you are no longer strangers and foreigners, but fellow citizens with the saints and members of the household of God.

We are considered adopted as children, heirs, and members in the same family! I don't know about you, but this makes me feel very special!

Please note that God calls Israel His *firstborn* (Exodus 4:22) and this is a calling they, as a nation, will always hold. When Gentiles trust in Messiah for salvation, they are called adopted and then are integrated into the community of the firstborn. However, there are promises that are unique to the Jewish people.

The next section is an excerpt from Sandra Teplinsky's book *Why Care About Israel* that explains the role of the believers in the tree.

Gentile Branches Save the Tree

If you are a Gentile Christian, you have been grafted into an olive tree, *the root of which supports you.* Paul says that God intends to graft the natural branches back in. Please don't let centuries of anti-Semitic training poison your heart and lead to your own branch being cut away. God wants you sharing in the roots' nourishing sap and blossoming instead. Let's see how.

When Paul penned his vivid olive tree metaphor, a horticultural practice in Israel was to invigorate an olive tree that had stopped bearing fruit by grafting wild olive branches into it. The fresh sap, or life-blood of the wild olive branches, would revive the cultivated tree, so the original branches could begin bearing fruit again. Meanwhile, the wild branches, formerly untended and unwieldy, flourished beautifully. What's more, with both wild and cultivated branches intermingled, the whole tree yielded such good and plentiful fruit as would otherwise prove impossible. When Gentile branches grafted into a Jewish-rooted tree function as God intends, the fruit is spectacular.

I have seen some gargantuan olive trees in Israel, hundreds or perhaps thousands of years old. Their gnarly roots span maybe half a city block, sturdily protruding above ground and firmly entrenched (as I suspect with my "city girl" understanding) until Messiah comes. Breathtaking in appearance, they grow knotty, wild and alone, bearing little fruit compared to the carefully planted and tended olive groves that dot the land.

I can imagine the Divine Husbandman gently lopping off a few branches from one of these untamed trees and hand carrying them to a failing cultivated tree. Next He cuts off some of the natural, cultivated branches, protectively setting them aside for future use. I picture Him lovingly linking the foreign branches onto the host, oozing a good dab of humility between them for His grafting agent. Then He blesses the branches and waits. Will this transplant "take"?

Jewish roots support new Gentile branches—but these engrafted branches are needed with their fresh vigor and vitality to save the whole tree. Now what if, for some reason, things go wrong and the Gentile branches sap rather than save the life of the tree? I suppose the Master could stand idly by, watching wistfully as the branches perish along with the tree they have choked. But that is not His nature; He will not let the tree die. I imagine He will have no real choice but to slice off and toss away those unruly engrafted branches.

Meanwhile, if the original tree is to bear fruit again, it must accept foreign, transplanted branches and freely share every bit of life it has with them. The two must become one for their mutual survival. God's grafting agent, *humility*, makes the miracle possible.

Jews and engrafted Gentiles must serve one another in a reciprocal flow of life not only to survive, but to bear "fruit that will last" (John 15:16). To put it more practically, Messianic Jews represent today's original, once-broken-off but now re-grafted, branches. We need lovingly reciprocal relationships of integrity with Gentile Christians. Just as much, Gentile churches need relationship with Messianic congregations and ministries. To produce fruit pleasing to the Master, we must learn (if that is what it takes) to serve one another in humility, for our destinies in Him are inextricably intertwined as one body.

Theologians have different—and good—interpretations as to the "root" of the olive tree. Some say the root refers to God Himself, some say the patriarchs, others say the faithful remnant of the Jewish nation, and still others say the Jewish Scriptures. I say, Why not *all* of the above? If you are grafted into the olive tree, God Himself is your portion, the Jewish Scriptures sustain your spirit and the Jewish patriarchs and people (most of all Jesus) offer you their legacy of truth. God wants the words of the Jewish Scriptures spoken to Jewish patriarchs and prophets to flow like nourishing sap through *every* branch in the tree.[5]

Just because we are grafted into the olive tree and we are considered adopted as sons, we do not have *all* the same benefits as Jewish believers. But we have equal salvation! I count that as a blessing that God would want *me* to be part of His elect!

We Are Indebted to the Jewish People

Since the days of Abraham, God has been dealing with the Jewish (Hebrew) people and preserving them (often just a remnant of them) to fulfill His promises to the world through them. We are indebted to the Jewish people for many things:

- Preserving God's Word, often hiding it and risking their lives. Paul said Israel is custodian of the Word of God (Romans 3:2).
- The covenants were given to them.
- Jesus said, "salvation is of the Jews" (John 4:22).
- We bear the guilt for their persecution as a race.
- Israel brought Jesus into the world.

---

[5] Sandra Teplinsky, *Why Care About Israel?: How the Jewish Nation Is the Key to Unleashing God's Blessings in the 21st Century,* (Grand Rapids, Mich.: Chosen Books, 2004), 119–121. Used with permission.

- Jesus, a Jew, brought the Church into the world.

God's Plan for Oneness

One of the most beautiful portions of Scripture tells us about the relationship God intended between Jewish and Gentile believers. God's plan is to have one family, made up of all those who receive Jesus as Messiah by faith— Jew and Gentile. It is a family made from every tribe, tongue and nation.

The New Testament explains God's desire that we would be one family. In John 10:15–16, Jesus makes this statement:

> "As the Father knows Me, even so I know the Father; and I lay down My life for the sheep. And other sheep I have which are not of this fold; them also I must bring, and they will hear My voice; and there will be one flock and one shepherd."

This discussion was with the Pharisees—a Jewish sect who carried on strict observances of the traditional and written law. They were considered self-righteous.

Jesus has sheep in the Jewish flock. The "other sheep" which are "not of this fold" are the Gentile believers. Gentiles are not in the Jewish flock. However, there will be one flock, and Jesus is the great shepherd.

Both the flock of sheep and the olive tree illustrate God's desire that Jewish and Gentile believers would be one family.

Our Responsibility to the Jewish People

In Romans 11:11–12, Scripture asks and answers the question: "Have they [the Jews] stumbled that they should fall? Certainly not! But through their fall, to provoke them to jealousy, salvation has come to the Gentiles." Gentile believers therefore have a responsibility to make the Jewish people envious. The purpose is that they will see strong and beautiful Gentile relationships with God and want the same. They should be scratching their heads that many believers know their Scriptures better than they do. They should be looking at us quizzically when we tell them we pray for them. They should watch with wonder as they see Gentile believers doing great deeds for others. But most of all, they should be absolutely jealous as they observe us exalting the name of God and worshipping Him with all of our hearts. They should hear about how blessed we feel because we have received the richness of salvation!

How Are We Doing?

Followers of Christ are called to bless the Jewish people (Genesis 12:3) and maintain a walk with Christ that causes Jewish people to be jealous and want Jesus Christ as their Jewish Messiah. Many Jews do not realize that Jesus is Jewish and loves them. He came for the lost sheep of Israel. Many Jews believe they must give up their "Jewishness," which is not true. Are you loving Christ so much that Jewish people are jealous of your relationship with their Messiah?

We are to integrate with Jewish believers, be grafted into *their* roots, bless them, and be one family with them.

Look how Paul cautions us in Romans 11:20–21:

> You will say then, "Branches were broken off that I might
> be grafted in." Well said. Because of unbelief they were

broken off, and you stand by faith. Do not be haughty, but fear. For if God did not spare the natural branches, he may not spare you either.

Sandra Teplinsky raises an important consideration regarding these verses: Here's how serious the stakes are…. "Does Paul imply that our right-standing with God, maybe even our salvation, is linked to our treatment of the Jewish people?"[6]

There will come a day when God will "…pour on the house of David and on the inhabitants of Jerusalem the Spirit of grace and supplication; then they will look on Me whom they have pierced; they will mourn for Him as one mourns for his only son, and grieve for Him as one grieves for a firstborn" (Zechariah 12:10).

In the end of days, "And so all Israel will be saved, as it is written: 'The Deliverer will come out of Zion, and He will turn away ungodliness from Jacob; for this is My covenant with them, when I take away their sins'" (Romans 11:26–27).

God will, without a doubt, continue with His plan for the Jewish people. While He is doing this, He has asked us to bless them and love them. If you are a Gentile Christian, you have been grafted into an olive tree—a tree with Jewish roots, intended to support you.

Paul is reminding Gentile Christians that trusting God also means joining His people. It is no different now than it was with Ruth:

Your people shall be my people, and your God, my God. (Ruth 1:16)

Gentile Christians have joined Israel—not the reverse.

---

[6] Sandra Teplinsky, *Why Care About Israel?*: How the Jewish Nation Is the Key to Unleashing God's Blessings in the 21st Century, (Grand Rapids, Mich.: Chosen Books, 2004), 112–113.

CHAPTER 5

The Appointed Days Illustrate God's Eternal Plan for Israel

In the book of Acts, we are told that Paul interrupted his missionary journeys to go up to Jerusalem for an "appointed time." The Sabbath and seven appointed times are a key component of God's commandments in Scripture in Leviticus 23.

Most Christians do not understand these holidays and even erroneously call all of them "Feasts." However, in Hebrew they are called *mo'edim* or "appointed times," and only some of them are actually feasts. In fact, one is a fast, or a day where Israel is told to "afflict their souls." These observances are important to Jewish people around the world.

Overview

The observances are given and described in Leviticus 23 in a specific order for prophetic reasons. On the Jewish calendar, they coincide with the two main harvest times in Israel: the barley harvest at the end of the spring and the wheat harvest at the end of the summer. They reveal great truths about the plans and counsel of the LORD God of Israel. They are all woven together like a beautiful tapestry and create a framework for the life of Jesus. Our calendar marks time, but the Jewish calendar is a testimony to God's work in their history and to the expectation of His work in the future.

Community is extremely important when celebrating these holidays. The memory of each occasion is kept alive over years and generations and establishes traditions. As each appointed time is celebrated, the Scriptural context becomes firmly embedded in the minds of the participants by the annual repetition. These observances can be thought of as rehearsals, much as a musician or an athlete, as he or she practices for an event.

The observances (appointed times) are tied to the calendar of the nation of Israel—to their seasons and to the passing of their history.

The appointed times point to:

- Jesus Christ (Yeshua)
- The founding of the Church
- The future of His people

The appointed times foreshadow God's completed redemptive purpose for Israel as well as His blessings to the Gentiles.

There are eight appointed times:

1. Passover (*Pesach*)
2. Feast of Unleavened Bread (*Chag HaMatzot*)
3. Firstfruits (*Bikkurim*)
4. Pentecost or Feast of Weeks (*Shavuot*)
5. Day of Trumpets (*Yom Teru'ah*)
6. Day of Atonement (*Yom Kippur*)
7. Feast of Booths or Tabernacles (*Sukkot*)
8. Sabbath (*Shabbat*)

The *one* observance that Christians believe is the biggest Jewish holiday is not on this list. Can you guess what that is? That observance is Chanukah, the Feast of Dedication, which is not one of the eight times appointed by God. Even so, Jesus celebrated Chanukah (see John 10:22–23). Chanukah commemorates the rededication of the Temple in Jerusalem, where the Jews sought to reestablish the freedom to worship which led to the Maccabbean revolt. Chanukah is observed for eight days and nights by the kindling of the lights of a nine-branched menorah.

Another holiday not included on this list is Purim. It is a Jewish holiday based on the book of Esther.

The Spring Feasts

The first four appointed times, the spring feasts, **point to the first coming of Messiah**.

1. Passover (*Pesach*)

There are three parts to this celebration: Passover, Unleavened Bread, and Firstfruits. Passover is the foundation for the others. A lamb was slain for deliverance of the household from death and from Egyptian slavery.

God delivered the Jewish people from their bondage in Egypt. In the final plague, God destroyed the firstborn of the Egyptians but spared those Israelites whose homes had the blood of a lamb smeared on the doorposts. God declared that the blood on the doorframes was the sign of faith He would accept to avoid death in a household. The Angel of Death would pass over those homes, hence *Passover*. Exodus 12:14 says this is to be celebrated "as a feast to the LORD; throughout your generations … as a permanent ordinance" (NASB).

Date: 14 Nisan, the first month of the Jewish calendar, which typically falls near the end of March.

History: God would remind them each year of Israel's slavery in Egypt (Deuteronomy 16:12). Israel was to celebrate their deliverance from Egypt, and Passover was an assurance to Israel that God would act on behalf of a faithful and obedient covenant people.

This is one of the three feasts God wanted celebrated in the central place of worship, the tabernacle, and later, in the Temple. Part of these observances (or holy convocations) required the males to go up to Jerusalem three times each year (Exodus 23:14-17). The first visit was to occur at the Passover season, followed by Shavuot (also called Pentecost), and then in the Fall the final visit during Sukkot, or the Feast of Tabernacles.

Scripture References:
- Old Testament: Exodus 12–13; Leviticus 23:5; Deuteronomy 16:1
- New Testament: John 1:29, 36; 1 Corinthians 5:7

Prophetic Fulfillment: Christ died for our sins. Jesus Christ is the Lamb of God. He is our "Passover" lamb who takes away the sins of the world (John 1:29). He is the final sacrifice. We are redeemed with His precious blood, as of a lamb unblemished and spotless, the blood of Christ.

In the New Testament, it was at a Passover meal when Jesus said the same thing about the New Covenant. His body was sacrificed and His blood poured out. Jesus told His disciples to eat this bread and drink this cup "'… in remembrance of Me.' For as often as you eat this bread and drink this cup, you proclaim the Lord's death till He comes" (1 Corinthians 11:25–26). Today we celebrate communion as a body of believers with that same purpose in mind. We are to remember the redemption that was paid for our sins all the days of our lives.

We can draw a few parallels: Passover was at the beginning of the Jewish religious year. When sinners trust in Christ, it is the beginning of new life. Israel was not only delivered from judgment; the nation was also delivered from Egypt and set free to go to their promised inheritance. Likewise, believers are delivered from judgment and set free to go to their promised inheritance.

2. Feast of Unleavened Bread (*Chag HaMatzot*)

In the seven days following Passover, the Jewish people eat only unleavened bread (that is, bread made without yeast) with their meals. Prior to Passover, they cleanse all yeast from their homes. In Scripture, leaven is symbolic of sin. Removing all leaven from the home is a picture of cleansing one's life of sin.

Date: 15–21 Nisan, around April

History: The celebration of Passover was to remind the Jewish people of the time when they had to leave in such a hurry that there was no time for their bread to rise—a reminder of their deliverance from Egypt.

On the first and seventh day of the feast, the people were to hold a sacred assembly. They were reminded of the Exodus because it was the greatest demonstration of God's deliverance in the Old Testament. God wanted His people to know and trust Him as the God who delivers. The focus is the same year after year.

God declared that eating the Passover meal with its special, unleavened bread was a sign of faith that indicated you were a true member of the covenant community of Israel. Christians refer to this today as *communion*.

> And as they were eating, Jesus took bread, blessed and broke it, and gave it to the disciples and said, "Take eat; this is My body." Then He took the cup, and gave thanks, and gave it to them, saying, "Drink from it, all of you, For this is My blood of the New Covenant, which is shed for many for the remission of sins." (Matthew 26:26–28)

A covenant meal was nothing new in the Middle East at that time. For centuries it had been understood that to eat bread with a man and share the same cup meant to make a very solemn and sacred commitment to him.

Scripture References:
- Old Testament: Exodus 12:14–20; Leviticus 23:6–8; Deuteronomy 16:8
- New Testament: 1 Corinthians 5:7-8, 2 Corinthians 5:21, 6:14–7:1, Philippians 1:21, 2:3–5, 3:8, 4:13

Prophetic Fulfillment: Jesus knew no sin, nor was any deceit found in Him. He was unblemished and spotless. He was made sin for us that we could be made the righteousness of God in Him.

> Purge out the old leaven, that you may be a new lump, since you truly are unleavened. For indeed Christ, our Passover, was sacrificed for us. Therefore, let us keep the feast, not with old leaven, nor with the leaven of malice and wickedness, but with the unleavened bread of sincerity and truth. (1 Corinthians 5:7–8)

Matzah or matzo (unleavened bread), has stripes. "By His stripes we are healed" (Isaiah 53:5). Matzah is also pierced. "They will look upon Me whom they have pierced" (Zechariah 12:10). Matzah is pure, without any leaven, as His body was pure and without any sin. The custom during Passover is to break, bury (fold in a white cloth and hide), then search for and, when found, "resurrect" the second of the three pieces of matzah (plural *matzot*), which is the middle piece, representing the sinless, second Person of the Triune Godhead, i.e. the Son. The Jewish people today thus act out Christ's resurrection and sadly don't recognize its significance!

The exodus of Israel in the Old Testament is an illustration of God's salvation. The crucifixion of the New Testament was the ultimate exodus, because it delivered not just from the bondage of a controlling Pharaoh, but from bondage to sin itself. It provides for eternal life—not just life in an earthly promised land.

Remember Jesus' claim to be the bread of life in John 6:35? Interestingly, He was born in Bethlehem, which, in Hebrew means the House of Bread!

3. Firstfruits (*Bikkurim*)

Following the Feast of Unleavened Bread, Firstfruits, also part of the Passover trilogy, acknowledges the fertility of the land God gave the Israelites. They were to bring the early crops of their spring planting and "wave the sheaf before the LORD" (Leviticus 23:11).

<u>Date:</u> There is some uncertainty about the date of this Holy Day, since the Scripture only defines it as "the day after the Sabbath." However, it is generally accepted that Firstfruits would begin on 16 Nisan.

<u>History:</u> The best of a barley crop was harvested first and dedicated to God, so they brought it to the house of the Lord. The first sheaf of the crop was presented as a wave offering before the Lord. It was a public acknowledgement that everything came from God and belonged to Him. The Israelites were not only to remember that the land was the Lord's and they were only tenants, they were to be aware that the fertility of the soil was not due to one of the foreign gods, but rather it was the Lord's gift to them.

The Jewish people were not allowed to eat of the harvest until the firstfruits had been given to the Lord. Proverbs 3:9–10 promises prosperity to those who honor God with the firstfruits.

<u>Scripture References:</u>
- Old Testament: Leviticus 23:9–14, 2:14–16; Deuteronomy 26:1–11; Numbers 28:26
- New Testament: 1 Corinthians 15:20–23

<u>Prophetic Fulfillment:</u> Israel was described as God's "firstfruits" (Jeremiah 2:3). Christ in His resurrection is described as the "firstfruits" of those that sleep/have died (1 Corinthians 15:20, 23). The first believers in Yeshua were also spoken of as "a kind of firstfruits" (James 1:18). Christ arose from the dead, having been lifted up, at the same time the barley sheaf on the Firstfruits ceremony was lifted up in the field, at the beginning of Firstfruits on Saturday evening, at the start of the first day of the week, Sunday. This was the fulfillment that Jesus is the Firstfruits of the resurrection.

The modern church has come to call this feast *Easter.* However, it is really the Feast of Firstfruits. Christ was raised from the dead, a living hope. Christ is the firstfruits of the resurrection with the promise of more to come. "But each one in his own order: Christ the firstfruits, after that, those who are in Christ at His coming" (1 Corinthians 15:23).

God accepted the sheaf as a symbol of the whole harvest, and because the Father accepted Jesus Christ, all believers are accepted in Him.

4. Pentecost or Feast of Weeks (*Shavuot*)

God gave us two of His most priceless gifts on this day: The Torah (His Holy Word) and the Holy Spirit. We need both—the Truth of God's Word *and* the Holy Spirit. But it is the Spirit that gives us the grace to live out that Truth in our daily lives.

Feast of Weeks marks the summer harvest or the wheat harvest. A wave offering consisted of two leavened loaves of wheat waved before the Lord. It is a day to give thanksgiving for God's *ongoing* provision for His people. A burnt offering of seven lambs, one bull, two rams, grain, oil, wine, a sin offering of a male goat, and a peace offering of two male lambs are also part of Shavuot.

Date: Fifty (*Pente*) days after Firstfruits, seven weeks and Sabbaths plus one day after the Feast of Firstfruits. It lasts one day. As for Firstfruits, the Scripture does not provide a specific date on the Jewish calendar for this feast; one must count off the fifty days. The Jewish people call this "the counting of the Omer." The counting begins with the wave offering of barley at Firstfruits and continues for forty nine days plus one, until the wheat offering on Shavuot.

History: According to Rabbinic tradition, Moses and the people received the Torah or Law at Mount Sinai on this day. Yet after receiving the Torah at Mount Sinai, three thousand Jewish people perished because of the sin of the golden calf (Exodus 32:28).

This is also the same day, centuries later, that God poured out the Holy Spirit on His followers, as they were praying in the upper room in Jerusalem (Acts 2). Instead of the priest waving sheaves before the Lord (as was done at Firstfruits), he waved together two loaves of bread baked with leaven, which were brought to the temple, symbolic of the eventual incorporation of Gentile believers (Acts 10) with the Jewish believers (both groups of sinful people forgiven on the basis of faith in Messiah) in His kingdom. This unity of the Jews and Gentiles is illustrated by the two leavened loaves waved together.

Believers were empowered that day to live a holy, Spirit-led life and to be His witnesses—in Jerusalem, in all Judea and Samaria, and to the ends of the earth!

Jewish people also made animal sacrifices as an offering to the Lord on this date. (Leviticus 23:18–19). No work was to be done on this day. This event would have marked the beginning of the wheat harvest (Leviticus 23:20–21), and the Jewish people were commanded to remember the poor as they harvested the grain God had generously given them. They were to leave the corners of the field for the poor and alien to glean. The traditional Scripture reading for Shavuot is the book of Ruth, reminding celebrants of her gleaning in the fields of Boaz.

Scripture References:
- Old Testament: Leviticus 23:15–21; Deuteronomy 16:9–12
- New Testament: Ephesians 1:13–14, 4:30, 5:18–27; 1 Corinthians 12:12–13; Galatians 5:22–23; Acts 2

<u>Prophetic Fulfillment:</u> Three thousand Jewish people—the same number that were lost after worshiping the golden calf (Exodus 32:28)—were saved after the Holy Spirit was poured out, and they were added to the community of believers (Acts 2:41). The Spirit of God reversed the destruction caused by the sin of man! This is the promise of the Holy Spirit and the mystery of the Church: Jewish and Gentile people united in one body.

The Spring appointed days (Feasts of the Lord) mentioned above had their prophetic fulfillment at the first coming of Jesus Christ, with His crucifixion (on Passover), burial (on Unleavened Bread), resurrection (on Firstfruits) and His sending the Holy Spirit (on Pentecost).

Note there is a jump in time from the Feast of Weeks or Pentecost in May or June to the next appointed day in the Fall, often in September. This seems to represent the Church Age that we live in now, in which we should be totally involved in the harvest and eagerly waiting for the sound of the trumpet (1 Thessalonians 4:13–18) to announce the Lord's Second Coming, which unquestionably represents the rapture of the Church prior to the second coming of Messiah.

The last three appointed times prophetically depict the future kingdom of God.

The Fall Feasts

5. Day of Trumpets (*Yom Teru'ah*)

Yom Teru'ah, renamed by the rabbis centuries later as the Jewish New Year (*Rosh HaShanah*, is literally "the head of the year," meaning its beginning. It is important to note that this differs from the "religious year," where God reordered the calendar in Exodus 12:2 to begin the year with Passover. This appointed time, though called the New Year actually is not in the religious sense. The trumpet was sounded on a variety of occasions in the ancient Jewish community:

- To announce significant events (Leviticus 25:9)
- To assemble Israel (Numbers 10:2)

- To obtain God's help against an enemy (Numbers 10:9)
- To call God's attention to an offering (Numbers 10:10)
- To announce the Presence of God (2 Samuel 6:15)
- To warn of war or danger

In Leviticus 25:10, God specified trumpets be used to "proclaim liberty throughout all the land, to all its inhabitants." That verse appears today on the Liberty Bell in Philadelphia, assuring us that America was founded by Bible believers.

I was a camp counselor for seven years at Indian Village, Forest Home. Each morning we were awakened to the loudest drum. At mealtimes, a smaller drum with a different beat was used. Different drum beats signified different events. Both could be heard throughout the camp so all would be aware of what was coming up. In the same way, the priests used a silver trumpet or a *shofar*, and the people knew what each sound meant.

The Feast of Trumpets is a one-day celebration in which no work is to be done and an offering is made to the Lord. The day is accompanied by trumpet (shofar) blasts.

<u>Date:</u> 1 Tishri, the first day of the seventh month, around mid-September

<u>History:</u> Over the years, the rabbis decided that the Feast of Trumpets marks the end of one agricultural year and the beginning of another and so they renamed it "Rosh Hashanah," the New Year. But the rabbis also recognized that the sound of the shofar on this day is an announcement of the upcoming Day of Atonement or Judgment (see below), and therefore the start of a time of introspection in which everyone is to examine themselves to see if they are living their lives in a way that is pleasing to God and, if not, to repent and to also try to heal any broken relationships with others.

<u>Scripture References:</u>
- Old Testament: Leviticus 23:23–25; 26:27–33; Numbers 10:1–10; Deuteronomy 28:58–67; Isaiah 11:1–12, 27:12–13
- New Testament: 1 Corinthians 15:51–53

<u>Prophetic Fulfillment:</u> The trumpet was a signal for the field workers to come into the temple. The high priest blew the trumpet so that the faithful would stop harvesting so as to worship. Now, when the trumpet sounds (according to 1 Corinthians 15:51–53), living believers will cease their harvest and rise from the earth. The church will be taken out of the world (in the rapture) prior to the day of judgment.

In 1 Corinthians 15:51–52 and 1 Thessalonians 4:16–17, Paul referred to the last trumpet and the trumpet of God. When Paul used these Hebraic expressions, he clearly had in mind the Feast of Trumpets as he described the rapture of the Church, making a deliberate connection between the rapture and the Feast of Trumpets. The trumpets mentioned in Revelation are not the same. We are talking here about the trumpet of God. In their book *The Last Shofar!* Joseph Lenard and Donald Zoller explain more about the significance of the Feast of Trumpets, which came to be known as the Feast of the Unknown or Hidden Day:

> Among the seven Feasts, The Feast of Trumpets is unique. Other Feasts were determined by calculating a stipulated number of days between the Feasts, based on the Jewish lunar calendar. Only the Feast of Trumpets is celebrated

on the first day of the lunar month and was determined by observing the appearing of the New Moon—that faint sliver of light indicating the beginning of the lunar cycle of waxing and waning. The possibility of obscured atmospheric conditions or poor human judgment to identify the appearance of the New Moon made the beginning day of the Feast uncertain—*the day and hour* unknown or hidden. In addition, orbital considerations of the relationship of the earth, moon and sun,...affected the observation of the New Moon.

To make matters more impacting, it is the appearance of the New Moon which determined the exact timing for the High Holy Days that followed the Feast of Trumpets, all occurring during the month of Tishri (the Days of Awe, *Yom Kippur* and, of course, the Feast of Tabernacles).

Consequently, the rabbis viewed the Feast of Trumpets with great concern and solemnity. To resolve this weighty problem, two witnesses appointed by the *Sanhedrin* were positioned strategically in different locations, waiting for the first indication of the New Moon. When the New Moon was sighted, the witnesses immediately reported their findings to the *Nasi*, the leader of the *Sanhedrin*, who *declared* precisely when the month of *Tishri* started, which officially determined when the *day and hour* of the Feast of Trumpets began. This was followed by a public declaration. Since no one knew for sure the exact *day and hour* when this Feast would begin, the Feast of Trumpets is referred to by the rabbis as the *Feast of the Hidden Day* (*Yom Hakeseh*).[7]

In Edward Chumney's book *The Seven Festivals of the Messiah*, he adds further understanding to this special hidden day:

---

[7] Joseph Lenard and Donald Zoller, *The Last Shofar!: What the Feasts of the Lord Are Telling the Church,* (Salem Publishing Solutions, Inc., 2014), 134-135. Used with permission.

One of the reasons most often given to disclaim that the resurrection of the dead and the catching away of the believers is on Rosh Hashanah (Feast of Trumpets) is the statement given by Yeshua in Matthew (Mattityahu) 24:36, as it is written, "But of that day and hour no one knows, no, not even the angels of heaven, but My father only." Because Rosh HaShanah was understood to be the hidden day, this statement by Yeshua is actually an idiom for Rosh HaShanah. Thus it should be given as proof that He was speaking of Rosh Hashanah because Rosh Hashanah (Feast of Trumpets) is the only day in the whole year that was referred to as the hidden day or the day that no man knew.[8]

Joseph Lenard and Donald Zoller continue their explanation:

The description of the Feast of Trumpets as being a Feast of an unknown day and hour—a hidden day—is inescapably similar to the words of Jesus, "But concerning that day and hour no one knows, not even the angels of heaven, nor the Son, but the Father only … Watch therefore, for you know neither the day nor the hour" (Matthew 24:36, 25:13 ESV).

As in most cultures, events are commonly referred to by using well understood expressions of association, i.e., the time when we decorate trees, sing carols and exchange presents is understood to mean Christmas in our culture. These are idioms which point us to a specific date on our calendar—our own Western feast day.

Likewise, when Jesus spoke to His disciples about when and how the age would end, He used a commonly understood idiom, i.e. "that day and hour no one knows," pointing them to the Feast of Trumpets and the subsequent events

---

[8] Edward Chumney, *The Seven Festivals of the Messiah.* (Shippensburg, Penn.: Destiny Image Publishers, 1994).. 138-139.

that introduced His Second Coming. This idiom was not lost on His Jewish hearers. Because of their heritage and the cultural setting of the Feasts, they clearly understood that the Second Coming of Christ was unavoidably connected to the Feast of Trumpets. This appears to be an essential piece of the prophetical puzzle![9]

6. Day of Atonement (*Yom Kippur*)

According to Leviticus 23:24, this is a day commanded that we meet together (a holy convocation) and a day to "afflict your soul," which may mean to fast from food or anything else that brings the body pleasure. It is meant to be a day to spend with the Lord. Yom Kippur is considered the holiest day in the Jewish faith.

It is a day of fasting and confession. The fast would remind the Israelites of Yahweh's holiness and their own sinfulness (including the high priest). It included a purification ceremony in the tabernacle and temple.

---

[9] Joseph Lenard and Donald Zoller, *The Last Shofar!: What the Feasts of the Lord Are Telling the Church*, (Salem Publishing Solutions, Inc., 2014), 134–136. Used with permission.

The Day of Atonement was the only time when the high priest could enter the Holy of Holies and call upon the name of God to offer blood sacrifice for the sins of the people (and himself). Sixteen sacrifices, thirteen burnt offerings, and four sin offerings were made. Two goats were placed at the entrance of the tent of meeting (tabernacle) where a high priest cast a lot, assigning one goat for God, to be sacrificed for a sin offering, but the other was placed before the Lord to be dedicated as a scapegoat and driven into the desert, carrying the guilt of Israel's sins.

Aaron confessed all the iniquity of the Israelites as well as their transgressions and symbolically placed them on the head of the scapegoat. The appointed person took the animal to the wilderness outside of the camp where he was to set it free (Leviticus 16:5–27).

When the priest came out of the Holy of Holies, the people rejoiced as they knew their sins had been forgiven for the year and that God's blessing rested on them.

Date: 10 Tishri, the seventh month, around late September

History: This is the day that the high priest would go into the Holy of Holies to present the offering of the blood of a bull and goat on the mercy seat to cover sins for the past year.

Scripture References:
- Old Testament: Leviticus 16:29–34, 23:26–32; Numbers 29:7–11
- New Testament: Hebrews 2:17–18, 3:1, 7–10

Prophetic Fulfillment: The high priest had to repeat the ritual of the Day of Atonement year after year, because the sacrifices only covered the sins of the people; they did not do away with them. However, Jesus Christ came at the right time (Galatians 4:4–5) and did what the blood of bulls and goats could not do. His sacrifice, His death on the cross, was the payment of sins and *removal* of guilt for mankind—once for all—no further sacrifices are required. The Day of Atonement reminds us there can be no salvation from sin apart from the shedding of blood (Leviticus 17:11). It also reveals the high priestly work of Jesus as our High Priest after the order of Melchizedek (Hebrews 5:10, 6:20).

The scapegoat mentioned previously is a picture of Jesus Christ as He had all the sins of the world laid on Him and removed our sins as far as the east is from the west. (Psalm 103:12) The second goat was sacrificed on the altar, just as Jesus gave Himself up on the cross as the ultimate sacrifice for our sins. Both goats are a foreshadowing of Christ because He took our sins away *and* He died for us. At the moment Messiah died, the veil in the temple was torn from the bottom to the top (Matthew 27:51). Now those who trust in Messiah can celebrate that their sins are forgiven *and* we have been invited to come boldly to the throne of grace with direct access—without priestly intervention (Hebrews 4:16).

The scattered nation of Israel will be gathered back into her land, and the sinful nation will be cleansed because they will recognize their rejected Messiah and repent of their sins. (Zechariah 12:10–13:1). It will be a national acceptance of Messiah. It will come when they say in Hebrew, *Baruch Haba B'Shem Adoni* (blessed is He who comes in the name of the Lord) Psalm 118:26, Matthew 23:39. The Old Testament sacrifices were a foreshadowing of the sacrifice of Messiah.

The Day of Atonement will be fulfilled in a wonderful way when Messiah returns at His second coming. He will restore the nation of Israel and then the final judgment of the world will occur.

7. Feast of Booths or Tabernacles (*Sukkot*)

During this seven-day celebration, no work was to be done on the first or the eighth day. In between these days of complete rest, offerings were to be presented to the Lord on each day of the seven-day period.

For one week, the people of Israel lived in makeshift booths of leafy branches, symbolizing their journey through the wilderness after leaving Egypt. The Feast of Tabernacles celebrates and reminds them of God's protection and provision in the Wilderness. This was to be a joyous celebration.

<u>Date:</u> 15–22 Tishri, five days after the Day of Atonement, near October

<u>History:</u> God wanted the people to remember that He provided shelter for the Israelites in the wilderness. Shelters or booths were to be built in which the people worshipped for the week of the feast to remind them of their departure from Egypt and their long journey to Sinai. They were to rejoice in the Lord during the entire celebration of the feast, giving thanks to God for His abundant gifts and all that He had done. This was the only festival where rejoicing is commanded by God.

<u>Scripture References:</u>
- Old Testament: Leviticus 23:33–44; Deuteronomy 16:13–17; Zechariah 14:16-19
- New Testament: John 1:14; 2 Corinthians 6:14–18; Matthew 25:21; 2 Timothy 4:1,8; 2 Peter 3:3–13; Revelation 20:4–6

<u>Prophetic Fulfillment:</u> This day reminded Israel of God's blessings in the past. He had led them out of Egyptian bondage, cared for them in the wilderness, and brought them into their promised inheritance. Once they had lived in booths and tents, but in the promised land, they would live in houses! Tabernacles represent the Lord's shelter in the future. Messiah will establish His future tabernacle in Jerusalem (Ezekiel 37:26) and the world will come every year to appear before the King and worship Him (Zechariah 14:16). A final ingathering will take place, a final harvest of Jews and Gentiles.

No nation in history has suffered as much as the Jewish people have suffered. But one day, their suffering will be turned into glory and joy. A great principle to remember from this is that joy always follows cleansing just as the Feast of Tabernacles follows the Day of Atonement.

For Israel, the best is yet to come! The scattered people will be (are being) gathered; the sinful people will be cleansed; the sorrowing people will rejoice. And for Christians, the best is yet to come: we shall be together with the Lord and His people, rejoicing in His presence!

During the thousand-year reign of Christ, families of the earth will come to Jerusalem to celebrate the Feast of Tabernacles (Zechariah 14:16–19). Afterward, there will be a new heaven and a new earth where God will dwell (tabernacle) with men (Revelation 21:1–3).

8. Sabbath (*Shabbat*)

The Jewish week (*shavua*) begins at sunset Saturday evening and ends at sunset the following Saturday evening. The Sabbath (*Shabbat*) begins Friday evening and ends Saturday evening. Scripture teaches that the *Shabbat* is the most important of the appointed days, since it is explicitly commanded to be observed in the Ten Commandments as a day when mankind is to remember God's creation of the world, after which He ceased from creation.

<u>Date:</u> The last day of every week, Sabbath, begins at sundown on Friday and continues until sunset on Saturday.

<u>History:</u> In Hebrew, *Shabbat* means "rest" or "cease from work."

<u>Scripture References:</u>
- Old Testament: "Remember to keep the Sabbath day holy" Exodus 20:8 (ISV)
- New Testament: Mark 2:27

<u>Prophetic Fulfillment:</u> The Sabbath points to the theme and goal of God's redemption program. It is a picture of rest. True rest comes through a relationship with Messiah. Weekly readings of God's Word are considered appointments with the Lord. A weekly Shabbat is not only a reminder of the rest our Messiah brought through salvation, but also a foreshadowing of the eternal security or rest we have in Jesus.

The Fall appointed days will be fulfilled at the second coming of Jesus with the rapture (Feast of Trumpets) and the physical return of Jesus to the earth to tabernacle with believers (Feast of Tabernacles) as well as the salvation of Israel (Yom Kippur).

A chart summarizing the appointed days and their Scripture references is in the Appendix.

Jesus celebrated these appointed times. They are reminders of what He has done for us in the past and they point to the future.

Appointed Time	Messiah's Calendar
To Remember Past Events	
Passover	Sacrifice of Jesus
Unleavened Bread	Sinlessness of Jesus
Feast of Firstfruits	Jesus Resurrection
Pentecost or Feast of Weeks	Jesus Sends Holy Spirit
To Point Toward Future Events	
Feast or Day of Trumpets	Jesus will call believers to be with Him
Day of Atonement	God will judge the earth
Feast of Tabernacles	Jesus will dwell with His people on earth

PART TWO

Historical Israel

CHAPTER 6
The Real Middle East Issues

On the same day, the LORD made a covenant with Abram, saying: "To your descendants I have given this land, from the river of Egypt to the great river, the River Euphrates ..." (Genesis 15:18)

Israel's Right to the Land

The Abrahamic Covenant is defined in Exodus 23:31— "And I will set your bounds from the Red Sea to the Sea of the Philistines [The Mediterranean], and from the desert to the River [The Euphrates] . . ." The land covenant God made with Abram, confirmed through Isaac and Jacob, was unconditional and everlasting (see Chapter 3, "Four Covenants Woven Together").

In truth, the Jewish people's rights to sovereignty over Judea and Samaria—as with their rights to the rest of the land of Israel—are overwhelming. From a historical and political perspective, during the 3,500-year political history of the land of Israel, the Jews were the only nation that viewed Israel as a single political unit, separate and distinct from all other territory, and as territory that uniquely served as their national, political, religious and territorial center.[10]

---

[10] Caroline B. Glick, *The Israeli Solution: A One-State Plan for Peace in the Middle East*, (New York: Crown Forum, 2014), 184.

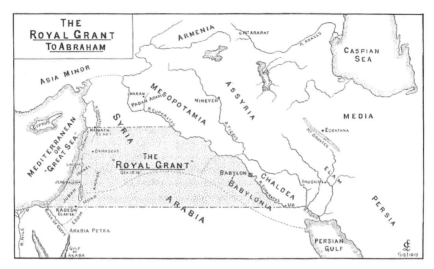

The Royal Grant to Abraham[11]

The Romans destroyed the temple in AD 70. After the Bar Kokhba revolt in 135 AD, the Roman emperor Hadrian changed the name of Jerusalem to *Aelia Capitolina*—a pagan city. He also changed the country's name from Judea to *Syria Palestina* (Palestine)—in an effort to wipe out any Jewishness in the land of Israel. He tried to connect the land association with Israel's historical archenemies, the Philistines, and erase evidence of Judaism from the Jewish nation. The name *Palestine* means "land of the Philistines."

After the temple's destruction in AD 70, the land was conquered by the Muslim armies of the Caliphate and Muslim presence in the region continued for nearly 1400 years. "In 1832 The Pasha of Egypt, Mohammed Ali, denuded the Holy Land of trees as he set out to build his ships."[12] The land became quite desolate during that time. Once sufficient tree root systems are gone, water can no longer be retained in the soil and desert-like conditions are formed. The land remained in that condition until the late 1800s. Mark

---

[11] Clarence Larkin, "The Royal Grant to Abraham," Blue Letter Bible, August 1, 2016, https://www.blueletterbible.org//study/larkin/lark03.cfm, Used with permission.

[12] "The Ottoman Period," in the *New American Standard Bible*, (La Habra, Calif.: The Lockman Foundation, 1995), 2096-2097.

Twain visited the Holy Land in 1867 and published his impression of its desolation in his book, *The Innocents Abroad*. He described a region devoid of both vegetation and human population:

> A desolate country whose soil is rich enough, but is given over wholly to weeds ... a silent mournful expanse ... a desolation ... we never saw a human being on the whole route ... hardly a tree or shrub anywhere. Even the olive tree and the cactus, those fast friends of a worthless soil, had almost deserted the country.

Time doesn't really allow for an indepth historical analysis of the events leading up to Israel's independence in 1948. However, there were a few significant events at the close of the 19th Century and the dawning of the 20th Century that set the stage for Jewish independence. Renewed attacks on Jewish communities in the 1880's, known as pogroms, awakened a sense for the need for the safety a modern Jewish state might provide. Jewish youth from Eastern Europe seized on old dreams of a nation state and from this was born the modern idea of Zionism. This also began the early immigration push into Palestine by these Eastern European Jews. These were known as "aliyot." These first waves of immigrants formed collective farms and a local defense force to protect them.

About that time, a political scandal captured French headlines concerning a Jewish military officer named Alfred Dreyfus. He was falsely accused of treason by the French government. The story was picked up by a young reporter named Theodor Herzl who brought the affair to international attention. This event, as much as any other, seemed to galvanize the international Jewish community towards the idea of accomplishing the dream. Herzl published his now famous work, Der Judenstatt (or the Jewish State) in 1896. Soon thereafter, a succession of international Zionist conferences framed the concept for a new Israel. Herzl travelled extensively and met with some of Europe's most influential leaders as well as attempting negotiations with the Ottoman Turkish authorities.

After Herzl's death in 1904, other attempts to establish the Jewish state eventually led to the publication of the Balfour Declaration, in 1917, at the request of the British queen.

The Balfour Declaration

The British acquired the land of Palestine (called the British Mandate) after the fall of the Ottoman Empire.

In 1917, Lord Balfour, Britain's Foreign Secretary, addressed a letter to Lord Rothschild, an influential member of the Jewish Community. The letter, known as the Balfour Declaration, said that the British government looked with favor upon the idea of a National Home for the Jewish people. Though a hotly debated topic for decades, the Jews certainly understood what a National Home meant.

World War I ended in 1918. Through a series of post-war conferences formed by the new League of Nations, the British acquired the land of Palestine, with the intent of administering the territory until its new inhabitants could accept and demonstrate the ability to govern themselves. This "British Mandate" was one of several created and put into action.

The British now recognized Israel's right to the land of Palestine (Israel), and the Balfour Declaration declared the establishment in Palestine of a national home for the Jewish people. Ever since, Jewish people have been "coming home." At the conclusion of World War I, the border of "Palestine" included not only lands west of the Jordan River, what we now call Israel, but lands east of the Jordan as well—all of modern-day Jordan and Israel.

Not long after the Balfour declaration was signed, the League of Nations met to settle affairs and apportion land to France and England, as well as the local inhabitants. Key members of the League, at the time the world's controlling international body, and the pre-cursor to the United Nations, signed a little-known document in San Remo, Italy, called the San Remo Agreement. This document "operationalized" the Balfour Agreement and created a Jewish state, at the time called Palestine (Grief, 38, 39).

In 1921, Great Britain gave up almost 80 percent of historic Palestine as a gesture to the Arabs and created Transjordan (which later became Jordan). Prior to this, there had never been a nation called Jordan, Transjordan, or even an Arab nation called Palestine. This was a brand-new nation for "Palestinian" Arabs living on the east bank of Jordan. In 1947, the United Nations recognized Israel as a state. Today, Arabs have their land in Jordan, yet they continue to hotly pursue a two-state solution in Israel.

See "Historical Timeline for Israel" in the Appendix for a summary of the history of the modern State of Israel.

Today, the hotspot in the news is always the Middle East. It has been for decades. Understanding the history of the Arab/Israeli conflict is imperative, yet it is also very complicated and volatile. Many have jumped too quickly on a bandwagon for support of one side or the other, without understanding the background. Books have been written on this subject and the purpose of this book is not to give a comprehensive report. However, some key points are beneficial to consider.

Every Muslim knows that Palestine was at one time ruled by Muslims. It was a Muslim-controlled territory (under the Muslim Turks and later the Muslim Arabs) and reverted by the decree of the U.N. resolution back to its previous owners, the Jews, in 1947.

Many Muslims today claim that once the forces of Islam conquer a land or territory, it is to remain under Islamic dominion forever ("for generations"), and it is a mortal affront to the supremacy of Islam when such territories would ever be lost to the dominion of Islam and revert to previous "infidel" ownership, as was the case in Palestine.

However, their own Qur'an states:

> Say: 'Lord, sovereign of all sovereignty. You bestow sovereignty on whom you will and take it away from whom You please; You exalt whoever you will and abase whoever You will. All that is good lies in Your hands. You have the power to will anything' (Qur'an 3:26).[13]

Arab/Israeli Conflict—Five Rejections and Two Failed Peace Talks

Five times the Palestinians were offered an independent homeland of their own in the West Bank and Gaza, and five times they rejected the offer. This Arab rejection has had disastrous consequences for both Israel and the Arabs.

1937 Peel Commission Partition—Rejected

Before Israel was even a state, the Balfour Declaration gave Britain a mandate over the land that was then called Palestine. Britain faced a problem that we still face today. There are two separate people groups—Jews and Arabs—claiming this little strip of land as their homeland. The British appointed the Peel Commission to investigate this situation and come up with a solution to the conflict. They decided that since there were two peoples in the same land, that they should split the land.

Rejection #1

---

[13] The Quran translated by Maulana Wahiduddin Khan and Farida Khanam, (New Delhi: Goodword Books, 2009).

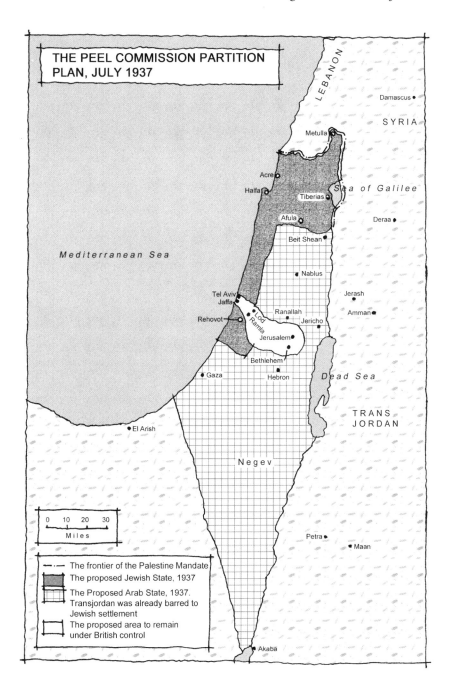

THE PEEL COMMISSION PARTITION
PLAN, JULY 1937

LEBANON

Damascus

SYRIA

Metulla

Acre

Haifa

Sea of Galilee

Tiberias

Afula

Deraa

Beit Shean

Mediterranean Sea

Nablus

Jerash

Tel Aviv
Jaffa

Ranallah

Amman

Rehovot

Lod
Ramla

Jericho

Jerusalem

Bethlehem

Gaza

Hebron

Dead Sea

TRANS
JORDAN

El Arish

Negev

Petra

Maan

| 0 | 10 | 20 | 30 |

Miles

–·– The frontier of the Palestine Mandate
The proposed Jewish State, 1937
The Proposed Arab State, 1937.
Transjordan was already barred to
Jewish settlement
The proposed area to remain
under British control

Akaba

The Peel Commission offered the Jews a tiny strip of land, much smaller than the present-day State of Israel—less than one-third of the land. The land was a tiny strip of coastal land where the city of Tel Aviv is located today and included the Galilee. There was a tiny section in the center that was going to be international. Everything else was to go to the Arabs as an Arab state. This was a generous offer. Around this time, the Holocaust was brewing, and the Jewish people were desperate for a land to call their own. The Jewish people agreed to the Peel Commission. However, the Palestinians rejected it. They refused, not because it wasn't enough land for them, but because they did not want a Jewish state anywhere in the Middle East.

What happened next is a part of history that is often forgotten. There was a huge British appeasement in 1939. After the Arabs rejected the Peel Commission plan, they began rioting because they didn't want any more Jews coming to live anywhere in the land of Palestine. They attacked British installations as well as Jewish communities. Britain's response to this Arab revolt was to appease them. The British recognized that the Arabs didn't want a Jewish state and didn't like Jews coming to live in their ancestral home, so Britain agreed to cut off or severely limit Jewish immigration when they issued the 1939 White Paper. The White Paper also provided for creating an independent Palestinian state.

Immigration basically came to a standstill, ending the Jewish return to their homeland. At this same time, in 1939 Europe, Adolph Hitler was trying to find a "final solution to the Jewish problem." When this White Paper was issued, Hitler did not yet want to kill Europe's Jews; he was still hoping to expel them. His first plan was to get the Jews out of Europe and send them somewhere else.

Hitler sent out a ship filled with refugees, the *St. Louis*, which was turned away from all the world's ports. Even the United States said *no*, causing the boat to go back to Europe. Many of those Jews ended up dying in the death camps.

There was nowhere for the Jews to go at this critical juncture in history. Britain had shut the gates of the Jewish homeland to any Jewish immigration. Although sources differ, virtually all sources agree that between nine to ten million Jews were, in effect, locked in Europe.

If the Arabs had agreed to allow that tiny little Jewish state, one-third the size of New Jersey, there would have been somewhere for the European Jews to go. The Arabs did not cause the Holocaust, but they, along with Britain, enabled the Holocaust to happen because they locked these Jews in Europe at a time when Hitler decided he had to get rid of them.

Annihilation, in his sick mind, became the only option.

The Jews agreed to the Peel Commission, even though the land was one-third of what they deserved, but they were desperate. However, the Arabs said *NO*.

> Consequences of Arab Rejection of the 1937 Peel Commission Partition:
> - Jewish immigration to Palestine was blocked or severely limited.
> - Six million Jews died in the Nazi Holocaust.

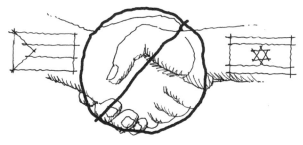

Rejection #2

1948 UN Partition Plan for Palestine—Rejected

After World War II, Britain realized they could not solve the problem of Jews and Arabs in the land known as Palestine. They decided to abandon the British Mandate and defer the decision about the land to the newly-formed United Nations and have them settle it. The United Nations deliberated, debated, and came up with the same solution that the Peel Commission had—two people groups were claiming the same strip of land—dividing it would be the only sensible solution.

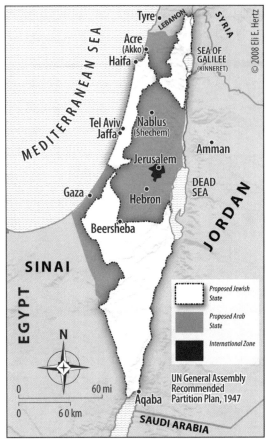

UN General Assembly Recommended
Palestine Partition 1947[14]

What the United Nations offered the Jews was a little better than what the Peel Commission offered. The lightest-colored section on the map is what was offered to the Jews, and the medium-colored area in the center and other sections on the map were offered to the Palestinians. It was about a fifty-fifty split. The Jews, in addition to that tiny coastal strip, were offered land in the Galilee and all of the Negev Desert. Most of what was offered to the Jews was desert. There was a "Special International Regime" for the city of Jerusalem.

Not only did the Jews say YES to this offer with its perceived limitations, they danced in the streets with joy. Finally, after two thousand years, they would have the right to return to their ancient homeland and have an independent Jewish commonwealth.

---

[14] UN General Assembly Recommended Partition Plan, 1947, provided with permission from Eli Hertz, www.MythsandFacts.org. Used with permission.

Rejection #3

Not only did the Arabs say *NO*, they took up arms to destroy this tiny Jewish state in its infancy. The Arabs attacked the Jewish areas and, within days, five surrounding Arab nations joined in the attack. Their attempt was to drive the Jews into the sea. They would not recognize *any* Jewish rights to the land; they would not tolerate a Jewish state in the land no matter how big or how small.

Many of these Jews had come to Israel out of displaced persons camps. They had survived the Holocaust. They had finally been allowed to return to the Jewish homeland. Many of them were getting off boats, still wearing their concentration camp uniforms because they had no other clothes. They were given guns and began fighting the invading Arab armies. Because of this war, over 6,000 Jews—1 percent of Israel's population at that time—died in Israel's War of Independence. That is an amazing price paid. In addition, 10,000 Jews were forced to evacuate their homes in Arab-dominated parts of former Mandatory Palestine. But a high price of the second Arab rejection was also paid by the Arabs living within Palestine, as they suffered many casualties

Consequences of Arab Rejection of the 1948 UN Partition Plan for Palestine:

- Over 6,000 people (1 percent of Israel's population) died in Israel's War of Independence
- Ten thousand Jews were forced to evacuate their homes, which were located in Arab-dominated parts of former Mandatory Palestine.
- Approximately 600,000 Arabs became refugees by their own decision.

and approximately 600,000 Arabs became refugees by leaving the area for the promise of an Arab victory.

1967 The Khartoum Resolution—Rejected

After the War of Independence—after Israel survived that invasion—Israel grew. However, relations between Israel and its neighbors never fully normalized. This led up to the 1967 Six-Day War.

By comparing the two maps below, you can see the difference in Israeli holdings before and after the Six-Day War. Their land included the south with the Negev Desert, the coastal land, and northern Galilee. Judea and Samaria (also known as the West Bank) had been held by Jordan in the War of Independence. Gaza on the southern coast had become part of Egypt after the War of Independence.

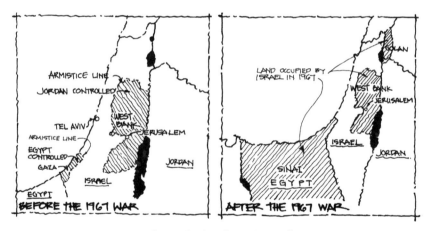

Before and After the 1967 War[15]

The map on the right indicates what Israel looked like after 1967 when the five Arab armies once again invaded Israel. Before that invasion, Judea

---

[15] UN General Assembly Recommended Partition Plan, 1947 provided with permission from Eli Hertz, www.MythsandFacts.org

and Samaria (referred to as the West Bank) was Jordanian and Gaza was in Egyptian hands.

Today, many look back at the war of 1967 and say the issue is "occupation." However, if the issue had been all about ending the "occupation," why did the Arabs invade Israel in 1967? If it's all about ending the "West Bank" occupation, why did the Arabs refuse Israeli statehood in 1948? Israel wasn't even offered the West Bank. If it is all about ending the "occupation," why did they refuse the Peel Commission in 1937, when Israel was not offered the West Bank? There seems to be a deeper trend here of rejecting a Jewish state in the Middle East, no matter how small and no matter where.

The Six-Day War began because Egypt cut off its straits to shipping and forced United Nations peacekeepers out of the Sinai. Israel pre-emptively bombed Egyptian airfields, causing Egypt, Syria, Jordan, and Iraq to attack Israel. However, things went well for Israel as she was able to liberate and reunify east Jerusalem.

In six days, Israel conquered the Sinai Peninsula, the Gaza Strip, the West Bank, and the Golan Heights in the north. In what seems a miraculous victory, Israel tripled its territory in just six days. Israelis really believed on the eve of that war that they were going to lose their state and lose their lives. They were terrified—but Israel vanquished its enemies in fairly swift order. Note that when Israel captured Jerusalem in 1967, it was not from Palestinians, but from Jordanians. Why didn't the "Palestinian" Arabs demand that *Jordan* give them their own state from 1948–1967?

What was Israel's first response after taking over the West Bank and Gaza strip? They offered to give it back to the Arabs in exchange for peace! Israel gained a victory—conquered land in a war that had been thrust upon them, yet their first reaction was to give some of this land back (even though it was important for their own defense). There never would have been an "occupation" if this offer had been accepted.

Rejection #4

But that offer was not accepted. The Arab League met the next month in Khartoum, the capital of Sudan. What was the Arab response to this Israeli offer? The response was the infamous "Three *NOs* of Khartoum."

The Arab League offered an official statement saying:

1. NO peace with Israel
2. NO negotiations with Israel
3. NO recognition of Israel

This Arab response is why Israel, unfortunately, began the official "occupation" of the West Bank, which is still an issue today. The Arabs wouldn't take it back as this would require negotiating with a state they didn't recognize. Israel was not inclined to hand over strategically vital territory to people still at war with her! Israel has been waiting for the day when the three *NOs* would turn into three *YESes*.

The following October, an Egyptian missile boat sank the Israeli destroyer *Eilat*, killing forty-seven people.

Consequences of Arab rejection of the 1967 Khartoum Resolution:
- Jews—Ongoing war, hostilities, terrorism
- Palestinians—"Occupation," West Bank Settlements

2000 Camp David Summit—Rejected

Keep in mind that Israel said they were going to hold onto this territory until the three *NO's* turned into three *YESes*. They were waiting for someone to take that land and live among them in peace—not live in the land and attack them.

By the 1990s, the Palestinians had developed a strong identity. It was no longer just a matter of their Arab neighbors leading the fight, but now the Palestinians themselves were leading the fight against Israel. The Israelis thought they saw a glimmer of hope. Egyptian Yasser Arafat, who created the Palestine Liberation Organization in 1964 before Israel even had the West Bank, who invented modern terrorism, who pioneered plane hijacking and massacres, said he was going to reject terrorism and begin negotiations. Israelis saw that as a historic moment. They rushed to the negotiating table. Israel placed on the negotiating table the West Bank, Gaza *and* East Jerusalem.

This process went on throughout the '90s. During these negotiations, Israel removed its troops from most of the West Bank and let the Palestinians rule themselves. For all intents and purposes, the "occupation" ended in the 1990s. This culminated in Prime Minister Ehud Barak's offer to the Palestinians at Camp David in 2000. The negotiations were based on an all or nothing approach—Nothing was considered agreed and binding until everything was agreed.

No maps were really presented in these negotiations. However, the Palestinians were offered the West Bank, Gaza, and East Jerusalem. This would end the "occupation" and they would have an independent Palestinian state. What was Arafat's response? No!

Not only did he say no, he also did not come back with a counter offer. Most Israelis and Americans criticize Arafat for the failure of the 2000 Camp David Summit. Many say that Arafat (and other leaders) were "performing" during negotiations to see how many Israeli concessions might be made to them without ever seriously intending to reach a peace settlement or signing anything that would end the conflict.

Immediately following the failed negotiations, Arafat began the intifada—a wave of suicide bombings against Israeli civilians, in which he competed with the terrorist group Hamas to see who could blow up more Jews and make themselves the champion of the Palestinian cause.

In summary, the consequence of the rejection of the offer by Ehud Barak to Arafat at Camp David was the beginning of the intifada, costing the lives of over one thousand Israelis killed in terrorist bombings. The price paid by the Palestinians in this rejection was also high.

At this point, Israel had vacated all of the West Bank. Counterterrorism depends on boots on the ground. You can't stop people from coming into Israel and blowing up busses and cafes unless you know there is an attack coming before the enemy travels a mile or two into Israel. Yasser Arafat refused to stop terrorism and, in fact, spent money to encourage it.

Israel had to go back into and re-occupy the West Bank and stop the aggression. Any responsible gov-

> Consequences of Arab Rejection of the 2000 Camp David Summit:
> - Jews—Over one thousand Israelis killed in the intifada
> - Palestinians—return of Israeli troops to West Bank, "occupation" resumed

ernment would do the same thing. In fact, they would have an *obligation* to do so. But, because of failed negotiations, Israel returned to the West Bank; the "occupation" resumed when it could have ended.

2008 Olmert's Peace Plan—Rejected

Again, Israel was holding onto this land for security purposes. They were basically forced to do this. They planned to hold on to this land until Arabs said YES—until they were willing to use the land for peaceful purposes and would pledge to refrain from attacking Israel.

Eight years after the failed Camp David Summit, Ehud Olmert, the prime minister of Israel, tried again. Yasser Arafat was dead, Mahmoud Abbas was the new Palestinian leader, and he seemed less bloodthirsty than Arafat and less committed to terrorism. Maybe someone would finally say YES to peace!

Olmert offered what Barak offered previously, and even sweetened the deal a bit.

Abbas just said *NO*. No one really understands why. It was thought this was what the Palestinians wanted ... an end to the "occupation" so they could have an independent state. What was wrong with this new offer?

Ehud Olmert offered Abbas everything you see on the map below in medium gray: all of Gaza, East Jerusalem, and all of the West Bank (except for the dark gray, not including Jordan, areas where Jewish communities were already established). The settlements to be annexed to Israel are designated in white. The areas to be transferred to the Palestinians are shown in black. Acre for acre, the trade was even.

Olmert's Peace Plan

On five occasions, negotiations broke off because the Arabs rejected the offers, even though they came to the negotiation table. There were many other occasions where both Arabs and Israelis signed an accord; however, the agreements did not hold for long. One example is the Oslo Accords.

> Consequences of Arab Rejection of Olmert's Peace Plan of 2008:
> * Jews—Continued "occupation in the territories"—no peace
> * Palestinians—Arabs living in "occupied territories"

1992-1995 Oslo Accords—Failed

The Oslo Accords are a set of agreements between the government of Israel and the PLO after representatives began secret talks in Oslo, Norway, in 1992. The Oslo Accord I was signed in 1993, while the Oslo Accord II was signed in Taba, Egypt, in 1995. Both were designed as confidence-building measures to create trust between Palestinians and Israelis. In exchange, the PLO agreed to stop incitement, renounce terrorism against Israel, and accept Israel's right to exist as a Jewish state within secure borders. At that time, both Israel and the United States decided not to focus on the PLO's terrorist past and acknowledged the PLO as the official representative of the Palestinian people. Israel agreed to withdraw from most of the Territories and to give the Palestinians self-rule.

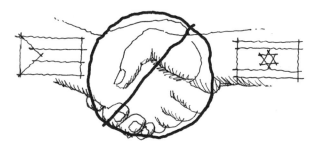

Rejection #5

Yet just a few years later, PLO Leader Yasser Arafat said to an Arab audience, "You understand that we plan to eliminate the State of Israel and establish a purely Palestinian state. We will make life unbearable for Jews by psychological warfare and population explosion … I have no use for Jews; they are and remain Jews."[16]

The signed agreements didn't have any better outcome than the five Arab rejections. Israel struggles today with the same issues they have had to contend with since 1948—Palestinian terrorism, Arab leaders renouncing Israel's right to exist, constant border attacks, etc. Meanwhile, since the Oslo Accords, Israel has given land to the Palestinians.

One such grant was the Gaza Strip, given under the leadership of Prime Minister Ariel Sharon. Shortly after the Palestinians were given the land, they turned it over to the control of Hamas, a terrorist organization which has regularly used the area to launch rockets into Israel. Hamas also enjoys easy access to Israeli-owned land for their terrorist assaults via their tunnels built from Gaza.

Abba Eban, an Israeli diplomat, coined the phrase, "The Arabs never miss an opportunity to miss an opportunity."[17]

When one understands that the Arabs and Palestinians are more concerned with destroying the Jewish State of Israel than they are about anything else, it is not surprising that multiple negotiations and even signed agreements have failed time and again. Since the five rejections, peace talks have come and gone with nothing new as a result. The most recent failed peace talks were 2013–2014, without any formal agreement on the table. Israel has fought several intermittent wars in 2008-2009 and 2012, with little success other than to suppress rocket fire temporarily from Gaza.

---

[16] Yasser Arafat, in the speech "The Impending Total Collapse of Israel", the Grand Hotel, Stockholm, Sweden January 30, 1996. Quoted in "Arafat in Stockholm," Arutz-7, February 27, 1996, online at http://www.professors.org.il/docs/stock.htm, as cited in *Israel 101*, a booklet produced by StandWithUs, www.standwithus.com

[17] Quoted by Khaled Diab in "Israel's Missed Opportunities," *Haaretz*, October 22, 2012, http://www.haaretz.com/opinion/israel-s-missed-opportunities.premium-1.471479.

2013-2014 Israeli-Palestinian Peace Talks—Failed

United States Secretary of State John Kerry attempted to restart the Israeli-Palestinian peace talks in 2013. Before the peace talks began, each side offered concessions. Israel was given a choice to either stop further expansion of settlements in the West Bank region or release 104 Palestinian prisoners.

Israel agreed to release the prisoners in waves as negotiations progressed. Some of those prisoners were responsible for killing 55 Israeli civilians. The Palestinians agreed to hold off pursuing international recognition as a state.

Some of the core negotiations issues that occurred during those talks involved borders, security, Jerusalem, refugees, settlements, and water.

During the negotiation process, Israeli Prime Minister Benjamin Netanyahu released all but twenty-six of the 104 prisoners, due to failed peace talks. Seventy-eight had been released in three waves.

A deadline of April 2014 had been set for agreement and on that deadline, negotiations failed. The reasons for failure are numerous. One reason that the Palestinians cited was that Netanyahu continued to expand settlements; however, freezing settlements was not a precondition to begin peace talks. Settlement expansion is not the reason for failed peace talks.

When Palestinian factions Hamas and Fatah formed a unity government, Israeli leaders suspended peace talks saying they "will not negotiate with a Palestinian government backed by Hamas, a terrorist organization that calls for Israel's destruction."[18]

> Consequences of the 2013–2014 Peace Talks:
> - Jews—Continued "occupation in the territories" and increased settlement building.
> - Palestinians—Sought and gained UN recognition. Fatah and Hamas formed a unity government. The Third Intifada was inflicted upon citizens of Israel, including knifings and vehicle attacks. Hamas kidnapped and killed three teenage boys, which triggered the 2014 Operation Protective Edge War.

---

[18] Attila Somfalvi, "Sanctions and suspended talks - Israel responds to Palestinian reconciliation," Ynetnews.com, April 24, 2014, http://www.ynetnews.com/articles/0,7340,L-4513046,00.html.

Netanyahu told Kerry, "I want peace, but the Palestinians continue to incite, create imaginary crises and avoid the historical decisions necessary for real peace."[19]

Do we expect peace now?

---

[19] "Netanyahu to Kerry: We want peace, but Palestinians continue to incite," *The Jerusalem Post*, November 6, 2013, www.jpost.com/Breaking-News/Netanyahu-to-KerryWe-want-peace-but-the-Palestinians-continue-to-incite-330763.

PART THREE

Political Israel

CHAPTER 7

Middle East Realities

Often, the hot topics in the news revolve around Israeli settlements, "occupied territories," apartheid, Holocaust denial, Jerusalem as Israel's capital, and refugees. If people are not properly informed, incorrect assumptions can lead to anti-Semitism. Middle Eastern news can be skewed, depending on the news source. Two reputable resources are *The Jerusalem Post* and *The Times of Israel*.

Below are statements that are erroneous, fictional, and hotly debated—followed by some history and truth which debunk these myths.

Israeli Settlements

> **Fictional Statement:** Israel's policy of building civilian communities (referred to as "settlements") in areas of the West Bank is the main reason there is no permanent peace between Israel and the Palestinians—and the reason for the failure of the peace process.

Settlement building is not the major barrier to a peace agreement. Two decades *before* 1967, when Jerusalem and much of the West Bank was controlled by Jordan, there were numerous terror attacks against Israel and no settlements even existed then. Terrorist attacks are nothing new and occurred long before any settlements were around.

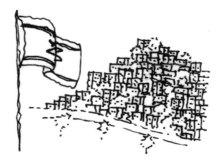

In 2005, Israel surrendered every single home, community, farm, business, and structure located in the Gaza Strip in hopes that the gesture would bring peace. It was called a "unilateral withdrawal" because nothing was pre-negotiated or gained by Israel in return for leaving Gaza—not even a promise for peace or a promise to negotiate.

Israel left the Palestinians with built towns and businesses, and the Palestinians destroyed all the free homes and buildings. This did not bring peace—the Palestinians launched thousands of rockets and engaged in numerous other terrorist attacks against Israel.

Today, if Israel agreed to no further settlement building in exchange for peace, the result would likely be the same. However, if Israel gave up the West Bank, the Palestinians would be closer to Israel's major commerce areas, ports, and the airports of Tel Aviv and Haifa. Attacks would be much more damaging.

> **Fictional Statement:** Israel has no right to occupy the West Bank at all.

Alan Dershowitz, professor of law at Harvard University, explains the situation this way:

> "On the basis of international law, this position is incorrect. Military occupations are clearly permitted under international law following an aggressive attack by a neighboring state. Jordan, Israel's neighbor to the east, attacked Israel in

1967, despite Israel's repeated efforts to keep Jordan out of the Six-Day War. In defending itself against Jordan, Israel captured the West Bank and the eastern part of Jerusalem. Under international law, until a meaningful peace is achieved and all terrorism against it ceases, Israel has every right to retain military control over this area. Since no peace treaty has been reached and the terrorism continues with new attacks threatened almost daily, Israel is under no legal obligation to leave.... military occupation is significantly different from building civilian settlements in a territory that is legitimately subject to a military occupation."[20]

Because Israel has built civilian settlements in areas marked as military occupation, some feel this has caused resentment and given cause to attack the legitimacy of the occupation in general. However, should Israel give up these areas of occupation, they would leave themselves wide open to terrorist attacks upon their largest industrial and business cities, Tel Aviv and Haifa. Dershowitz explains further:

While the settlements may have contributed to the difficulty of making peace, it has not been the major barrier that Israel's enemies claim them to be. It is not the reason there has been no peace agreement between Israel and the Palestinians. The reason has always been and remains the unwillingness of Palestinian leaders … to recognize Israel's right to exist as the nation state of the Jewish people. Until and unless the Palestinian leadership and the Palestinian people acknowledge that the State of Israel has the right to be free from:

- Military Assault
- … Terrorism

[20] Alan Dershowitz. "Are Israeli Settlements the Barrier to Peace?" Prager University video, 4:32. January 12, 2015. https://www.youtube.com/watch?v=dhbCtAz_BQc&feature=em-subs_digest.

- • … Rocket Attacks
- • … Diplomatic Warfare

… there will be no resolution to the Middle East dispute.

If these conditions, which must be the basis of any two-state solution—meaning a nation State for the Jewish people and a Palestinian State, are met, the occupation will end, the settlement issue will be resolved, and the blessings of a mutual peace will finally be achieved."[21]

However, the Oslo Accords do not prohibit Israel from building homes or "settlements." According to international law, the status of the settlements is "disputed," though the media routinely defines it as "occupied Palestinian territory."[22] Palestinian President Mahmoud Abbas has also "acknowledged that settlements take up approximately 1.1 percent of the pre-1967 West Bank territory. Yet, as Abbas flagrantly violated the Oslo Accords with his UN bid, the media reinforced the fable that settlements "eat away at land meant for a future Palestinian state."[23]

Israel holds that the last legal claims to this land were included in the British Mandate, which was the last legal sovereign authority for the territories. Jordan and Egypt illegally held them between 1948 and 1967. They remain unallocated portions of the British Mandate, since no government formally replaced the Mandate's jurisdiction. Its guidelines called for Jews to settle the area.[24]

Israel also has historical claims: Judea and Samaria (renamed the West Bank by Jordan in 1951) were the cradle of Jewish civilization and had a

---

[21] Ibid.

[22] Michelle Whiteman, "To the Media, Building Settlements in Israel's a Crime," *Huffington Post,* December 26, 2012, http://www.huffingtonpost.ca/michelle-whiteman/israeli-settlements-west-bank_b_2316941.html.

[23] Ibid.

[24] British Mandate for Palestine, League of Nations, September 29, 1922

continuous Jewish presence until the 1948 War when Jewish inhabitants were killed and approximately ten thousand were expelled by the Jordanians.[25]

The media continues to misrepresent the issue of settlement building as an obstacle to peace. The real issue is not settlements. The real obstacle to peace is that the Palestinians will not recognize Israel as a Jewish state.

The "Occupied Territories"

The first use of the term "territories occupied" was in the United Nations Security Council Resolution 242 after Israel's defensive Six-Day War in 1967. The term implies an aggressive effort to take over and rule a foreign people.

Arab states and Palestinians refused to accept the Jewish state's right to exist and mobilized again to destroy it. As Israel defended itself, it drove back Jordanian, Egyptian, and Syrian troops and captured the territories that fell on Israel's side of the armistice lines. These territories included the West Bank (including Jerusalem), much of the Golan Heights, the Gaza Strip (given up in 2005) and, until 1982, the Sinai Peninsula. Israel wanted to give the land back in exchange for peace, but in 1967 the Khartoum Resolution was rejected, leaving Israel in control of the territories.

Later, the rejection of the Olmert Peace Plan of 2008 left Israel still occupying these lands. The so-called "occupation" continues to this day because all other efforts to negotiate peace have been rejected by the Palestinians.

Apartheid

> **Fictional Statement:** To create Israel, the Jews had to kick out and expel Palestinians from their land. "Israel is an apartheid state."

Apartheid is a former social system in South Africa in which black people and people from other racial groups did not have the same political and economic rights as white people and were forced to live separately from white people.

---

[25] Anita Shapira, "The Past is Not a Foreign Country: The Failure of Israel's 'New Historians' To Explain War and Peace," *The New Republic*, November 29, 1999.

Many have applied the term *apartheid* to Israel, comparing its treatment of the Arabs living there to the treatment of non-whites by South Africans, implying that Arabs do not have the same rights as Jewish Israelis and have been separated from the others in Israel.

The Arab population in Israel is 1.5 million, 20 percent of the population. Arab citizens have the same rights as Jewish citizens. They may vote, own property and businesses, serve in the Israeli parliament, serve as judges, and work alongside other Israelis. Arabs occupy senior positions in all sectors of Israeli society. For example, Arab members of the 2015 Knesset included Zouheir Bahloul, Issawi Frej, Basel Ghattas (a Christian Arab), Masud Ghnaim, Yousef Jabareen, Ayoob Kara, Ayman Odeh, Osama Saadi, and Ahmad Tibi.

Not all Arabs hate Israel. In fact, many living in Israel view their life in Israel as better than living in any Arab state. Arabs in Israel are freer than in any other country within the Arab world. Israel is a liberal democracy that respects civil rights. One study found that 82 percent of Israeli-Arabs would rather be citizens of Israel than any other country.[26]

For the testimonial of one Arab woman living in Israel, please view this Facebook video: https://www.facebook.com/mirilavi/videos/10154126499312715/.

On the other hand, Palestinians living in the "occupied territories" are treated differently because they are not citizens of Israel. They are governed by either the Palestinian Authority or Hamas. Media will often distort the truth and state that Palestinians living in Israel do not have the same rights as Jewish Israelis. This is only true if they live in the "occupied territories" governed by Palestinian leaders.

Because of this, those who hate Israel hope to persuade uninformed people that Israel does not deserve to exist. These haters are persuaded to act out against Israel by becoming part of the Boycott, Divestment, and Sanctions (BDS) Movement or Israeli Apartheid Week. (See chapter 10.)

Every year college campuses across the country hold a festival of hatred

---

[26] Uzi Arad and Gal Alon, "Patriotism & Israel's National Security" (working paper, Institute for Policy & Strategy, Lauder School of Government, Diplomacy & Strategy, Herzliya, Israel, 2006).

aimed at Jews and the Jewish state. Israeli Apartheid Week has become notorious for the targeted harassment of Jewish students, support for Hamas, and even physical violence.

When you hear it said that "Israel is an apartheid state," remind the speaker that all Israeli citizens have equal rights—Arabs as well as Jews—and many Arabs hold government positions. These things would not happen in an apartheid state.

Holocaust Denial

> **Fictional Statement:** The Holocaust never happened. It is a hoax arising out of a deliberate Jewish conspiracy to advance the interest of the Jews at the expense of others.

Holocaust denial is an anti-Semitic propaganda movement active in the United States, Canada, and Western Europe that seeks to deny the reality of the Nazi regime's systematic mass murder of six million Jews during World War II. It generally depicts historical accounts of this genocide as propaganda, generated by a Jewish, or "Zionist," conspiracy.[27]

---

[27] "Fight Anti-Semitism," Anti-Defamation League, http://archive.adl.org/hate-patrol/holocaust.html#.VbF0yPlVhBc

The Anti-Defamation League's Global 100 survey said, "Nearly 70 years after the end of World War II, awareness of the Holocaust is alarmingly low in many parts of the world. Even more disturbing is the percentage of people who have heard of the Holocaust but think it is either a myth or that the number of Jews who died has been greatly exaggerated."

The ADL survey found that 54 percent of the people of the world have heard about the Holocaust; 32 percent of people who have heard about the Holocaust think it is either a myth or has been greatly exaggerated.[28] Here is a chart of their findings:

Holocaust Awareness or Denial by Region

Region	Heard of Holocaust	Myth/Exaggeration
Australia	93%	8%
Western Europe	94%	11%
The Americas	77%	21%
Eastern Europe	82%	24%
Asia	44%	41%
Africa	24%	44%
Middle East & North Africa	38%	63%

Source: The ADL Global 100

The proof of the killing of nearly 6 million Jews has been a matter of public record since late 1945 and is available in libraries around the world. Below is a chart indicating Jewish Holocaust victims by country.

[28] "The Holocaust—Global Awareness and Denial," The ADL Global 100, 2015, http://global100.adl.org/info/holocaust_info

Jewish Victims of the Holocaust[29]

Country	Minimum Loss	Maximum Loss	% of Jewish Population
Austria	50,000	50,000	27%
Belgium	28,900	28,900	44%
Bohemia & Moravia	78,150	78,150	66%
Bulgaria	0	0	0%
Denmark	60	60	0.7%
Estonia	1,500	2,000	44%
Finland	7	7	0.3%
France	77,320	77,320	22%
Germany	134,500	141,500	25%
Greece	60,000	67,000	86%
Hungary	550,000	569,000	69%
Italy	7,680	7,680	69%
Latvia	70,000	71,500	78%
Lithuania	140,000	143,000	85%
Luxembourg	1,950	1,950	56%
Netherlands	100,000	100,000	71%
Norway	762	762	45%
Poland	2,900,000	3,000,000	90%
Romania	271,000	287,000	47%
Slovakia	68,000	71,000	80%
Soviet Union	1,000,000	1,100,000	36%
Yugoslavia	56,200	63,300	81%

Source: The National World War II Museum

As many as five million non-Jews—people seen as enemies of the Third Reich—were also killed in the Holocaust, including Communists, Roma [Gypsies], Serbs, Polish intelligentsia, political opponents, resistance fighters, homosexuals, Jehovah's Witnesses, and the physically and mentally disabled.

---

[29] The National World War II Museum, New Orleans (www.nationalww2museum.org/learn/education/for-students/ww2history/ww2-by-the-numbers/holocaust.html), 945 Magazine Street, New Orleans, LA 70130

For people to argue that the Holocaust never happened is ridiculous. The proof has been documented repeatedly. I have personally heard testimonies of over twenty Holocaust survivors. Any time I hear that Holocaust survivors are sharing their testimony, I make a point to go meet them, and encourage the generation after me to do the same.

Picture from Yad Vashem Holocaust Museum, Israel. Photo by Deby Brown.

Jerusalem as Israel's Capital

Fictional statement: Jerusalem will never be the capital of Israel exclusively.

Jerusalem is one of the key issues in the Israeli-Palestinian peace process. Both the Israelis and the Palestinians want to claim it as their capital.

When Israel gained statehood in 1948, they declared Jerusalem as their eternal and undivided capital. However, Arab nations immediately attacked her and captured Jerusalem. During the Six-Day War in 1967, Israel liberated Jerusalem.

Today, Israel claims Jerusalem as its united capital, with most branches of Israeli government headquartered there, including the Knesset building. Only the Ministry of Defense is located in Tel Aviv rather than Jerusalem.

However, Israel's recognition of Jerusalem as its capital has not been echoed internationally. The Palestinian National Authority views East Jerusalem as occupied territory.[30] The Palestinian Authority claims all of East Jerusalem (including the Temple Mount) as the capital of the state of Palestine. In addition, it claims that West Jerusalem is also subject to permanent status negotiations.

The United Nations General Assembly does not recognize Israel's proclamation of Jerusalem as the capital of Israel. The UN is holding out to make it an international entity. The United States desires that an international regime be established for the city and that its status must be resolved through negotiations. Therefore, the U.S. has not recognized Jerusalem as Israel's capital and keeps its embassy in Tel Aviv, with only a consulate in Jerusalem.

The Palestinians envision East Jerusalem as the capital of their future state. For Palestinians, Jerusalem is their third holiest city, second only to Mecca and Medina. Jerusalem is home to the Dome of the Rock and the al-Aqsa Mosque, commemorating Mohammed's night of ascension. However, the city seems to have become more popular with Islam only since the advent of Zionism.

Most Israelis remain adamant that the city will never again be divided.

Jerusalem is where the Jewish Temple Mount stands, awaiting its future Third Temple, which the Bible clearly claims will be built. It is the place where Abraham offered Isaac and where Gideon threshed wheat. It is the place where Jesus went to temple and taught and where sacrifices to a Holy God were offered. It is where God said, "...In Jerusalem I will put My name." (2 Kings 21:4b) The LORD had said to David and to Solomon, "... "In this house and in Jerusalem, which I have chosen out of all the tribes of Israel, I will put My name forever." (2 Kings 21:7b) Revelation chapters 21 and 22 speak of the day that the New Jerusalem will be the undisputed capital of Israel.

As of the writing of this book, President Donald Trump of the U.S. has promised that he will move the American Embassy from Tel Aviv to

---

[30] United Nations Security Council Resolution 242

Jerusalem, affirming Jerusalem as Israel's capital. However, the Palestinians warn Israel that should the embassy move to Jerusalem, that act will end the peace process.

Refugees

> **Fictional statement:** Israel is the cause for 1.1 million Palestinians being displaced and living today as refugees.

Both Jews and Arabs became refugees after the 1948 War of Independence. Over 10,000 Jews became refugees, coming from areas of the Palestine Mandate, but you don't hear about those people today. Both Jews and Arabs were welcomed back to the State of Israel as full citizens, and two-thirds of them accepted that invitation and settled in Israel. The other one-third settled in other nations. In addition, there were more than 700,000 Arabs whose leaders forbade them from settling in the new State of Israel. As a result, today there are still more than 1.1 million "Palestinian refugees" living in neighboring Arab countries. This was the price paid by the Palestinians because of their refusal to recognize Israel as a state. Interestingly, Israel accepted any Jews who left these Arab nations as full citizens and continues to do so.

> Wars create refugees. If Arab leaders had accepted the UN Partition plan instead of launching a war to seize the whole British Mandate, today an independent Palestinian-Arab state would exist alongside Israel. There would have been no Palestinian refugees. If Arab countries had not expelled their Jewish citizens, there would have been no Jewish refugees from Arab countries, either.[31]

As discussed in the previous chapter, the refugee problem is not generated by Israel. The problem was and is fueled by Palestinians. They will not

---

[31] Israel 101 booklet, produced by StandWithUs, p. 14. For a free electronic copy, go to www.standwithus.com.

let the refugees and their families become citizens in their land of Gaza that was given to them. They also will not allow Palestinian refugees to become Jordanian citizens as they pose a demographic threat.

The reason there are Palestinian refugees is because of the rejection of the UN Palestine Partition in 1948 which led to a war in which Arab refugees fled out of fear of war. In a Prager University video called "Born to Hate Jews," Kasim Hafeez cites an Alan Dershowitz book, *The Case for Israel*, saying, "It wasn't Israel that created the Palestinian refugee crisis; it was the Arab countries, the United Nations, and the corrupt Palestinian leadership."[32]

When the UN agreed to the partition plan—when Israel declared its independence—with those lines drawn by the UN (see previous chapter), there was not one refugee. The Jewish cities were built on land that was legally theirs. Communities were built. Tel Aviv was built on what had been sand dunes. *No one* had ever lived there before. There was not one Arab refugee at

---

[32] Kasim Hafeez. "Born to Hate Jews." Prager University video, 4:45. December 5, 2016. https://www.prageru.com/courses/political-science/born-hate-jews

this juncture. Had the Palestinians agreed to this UN Partition Plan, there would never have been one single Palestinian refugee.

But the Palestinians and five Arab countries invaded and tried to destroy the State of Israel. Arabs fled when they heard bombs and guns. Records have been found of radio announcements in which Arab leaders got on the radio and pleaded with their Arab brothers to flee from their villages that were near the Jews because Arab fighters were coming to drive the Jews into the sea. The announcements assured them that they could return to reclaim their homes as well as homes previously owned by Jews.

In addition, Arab leaders admit that they blamed Jews for raping women and children—which was a lie. Arab radio stations covered this news, ignoring reports of witnesses. They felt that they had to spread this lie so that Arab armies would come to liberate Palestine from the Jews. They admit this was the biggest mistake they made. They did not realize how their own people would react to this news. When the people heard women and children had been raped, they fled their villages in terror. Half of the Arab population (more than 700,000 people) fled from their homes in Palestine. Israel never allowed them back.[33]

Israelis also committed some atrocities at this time. When some Israelis committed violence, Arabs fled in fear. This was not a war of Jewish aggression, but one that was forced upon this tiny Jewish state. It is a miracle that the state survived.

According to the United Nations Relief and Works Agency (UNRWA) website, Gaza Strip today is home to a population of more than 1.5 million people, including 1.1 million Palestinian refugees. A logical question would be, "Why are there 1.1 million Palestinian refugees living in Gaza today when the refugee situation began in 1948?" The answer is that the Palestinian leaders desire that the refugees remain refugees until Arabs conquer Israel as their own land. Many Arab nations are wealthy, so it is not a matter of finances. Meanwhile, those living under refugee conditions receive funding from the UNRWA for Palestine refugees in the Middle East.

---

[33] *The 50 Years War—Israel and the Arabs,* directed by David Ash and Dai Richards (Warner Bros., Brian Lapping Associates, and WGBH Educational Foundation, 1999), DVD.

In 1949 the UN set up UNRWA, an agency exclusively serving the Palestinian refugees. Their website claims "We provide assistance and protection for some 5 million Palestine refugees."[34] Obviously, they are considering descendants—four generations—as refugees. No other group's descendants are also considered refugees.

During a visit to Israel in July 2015, I travelled for hours along a road that was about two miles from Gaza and noticed many UNRWA trucks with supplies entering the Gaza area, while just as many were returning from Gaza empty. I asked about this and was informed that at least one hundred trucks filled with supplies (most from UNRWA) are sent to Gaza daily to meet the needs of the refugees. Where does the money come from?

UN member states fund the UN, which then donates money to the UNRWA. The USA is a member state, so some of your tax money goes to the UN and directly funds relief for Palestinian refugees. Before you get upset about that, don't be angry with the refugees. It is not their fault that they have been considered "refugees" for sixty-nine years. The Palestinian leaders have kept their people oppressed in this situation. We absolutely should hold the Palestinian leaders accountable for this, as it is inhumane and unfair.

Today, the refugees of Gaza have been awarded special treatment by the UN. Even Israel has contributed money to UNRWA, but neither the USA nor Israel have any control over how the money or supplies are used once given. It has not always been used with the stated intentions. In fact, the PLO and the UN denounced improvements to refugee housing (UNGA Resolution 2792). The Palestinian refugees have and continue to be manipulated as political pawns, yet Israel is blamed.

This chapter was not intended to go into great depth regarding each of these issues, but to whet your appetite, hoping that you will continue to do your own research. These are extremely important issues that you need to understand so that when they come up in conversation, you will be girded with the truth (1 Peter 3:15).

---

[34] United Nations Relief and Works Agency for Palestine Refugees in the Near East, home page, accessed April 26, 2017, www.unrwa.org.

CHAPTER 8

Do We Expect Peace Now?

On five key occasions, a Palestinian state has been offered—and five times the Palestinians have rejected the offers.

Israeli Prime Minister Netanyahu attempted to restart peace talks in 2011. He pleaded with the UN and with Palestinian Authority President Abbas to meet without any preconditions. Abbas refused and demanded that Israel first agree to an expanded list of preconditions.

> A Palestinian State has been offered—and rejected:
> - 1937 by the Peel Commission
> - 1948 by the United Nations
> - 1967 after the Six-Day War
> - 2000 by Ehud Barak
> - 2008 by Ehud Olmert

After reviewing history, we ask these final questions: Is a sixth offer to the Palestinian president the key to peace this year? Is Israel the barrier to peace? If Israel makes a sixth offer, will there finally be peace in the land? Or is there a deeper and more difficult problem?

Most Americans and Israelis believe in their hearts that the solution will come about through negotiation. Many believe that a two-state solution is the answer. However, there is this deeper problem of the Arabs rejecting a Jewish state anywhere in the Middle East. This is what has driven the conflict from the beginning and what is driving it today. When people portray Israelis as the obstacle, one wonders if they understand this history and the truth.

West Bank Map[35]

---

[35] U.S. Central Intelligence Agency's World Factbook, https://www.cia.gov/library/publications/the-world-factbook/ Used with permission.

The West Bank has cities with Hebrew names. Some are Judea, Samaria, Hebron, Bethlehem, and Jericho. Most of the stories in your Bible about the Jews and their homeland took place in the West Bank. This land is precious to the Jews. Israel has reluctantly given away some of these cities in exchange for peace. Jerusalem is in the center of this area. It is the most important area for every religious Jew and for Christians as well. The West Bank is also strategic land, being mountainous. The West Bank overlooks the most important areas of Israel today—Tel Aviv (Israel's second-largest city and the twenty-fifth most important financial city in the world) and Haifa (Israel's third-largest city, a major seaport, and a center of heavy industry), for example. The West Bank is really the biblical heartland of Israel.

The coastal strip is where the Phoenicians—the Philistines—lived. They didn't live in the hills.

Gaza, in the lower region, has been run by Hamas since 2007. Hamas is a terrorist group that has openly vowed to destroy Israel. When Israel gave up Gaza, they gave it to the Palestinians—not Hamas. It was immediately taken over by Hamas—in only one week—and Hamas uses it to fire missiles into southern Israeli cities.

What if Israel gives the West Bank to Palestinians? Will they quickly give control over to Hamas for the destruction of Israel? Then they could fire missiles from the West Bank into Jerusalem, Tel Aviv, and Haifa.

When you come to Israel's defense, you may encounter two myths which foster discord based on erroneous accusations.

> **Myth 1:** To create the State of Israel, the Jews had to kick Palestinians out of their land.

> **Myth 2:** If Israel would end its occupation of the West Bank and allow the creation of a Palestinian state, there would be peace in the Middle East.

In other words, Palestinian sympathizers wrongly claim that Israel is driving this conflict, occupying the Arab land, and prohibiting the formation of a Palestinian state.

You may have great sympathy for Palestinians who want their own land. The Palestinians have a right to be angry. But they should not be angry with Israel. They should be angry with their own parents, grandparents, and leaders. Israel has offered the Palestinians a Palestinian state on five separate occasions and five times the offers were turned down.

From a Palestinian Perspective

I met Taysir Saada at a gathering in a home where he told his amazing life story. Taysir, known as Tass, was born in a Palestinian refugee camp in Gaza in 1951. When he was only a few months old, UN authorities sent his family to Saudi Arabia, where they continued to live as refugees. At 17 years old, Tass left his home to become a Fatah sniper in Gaza. He was promoted to assassin and eventually became Yasser Arafat's chauffeur.

Through very unusual circumstances, Saada was introduced to Jesus Christ and experienced a radical transformation. His story is an amazing testimony of how God can change a Jew-hating heart to one of love, with a desire that Arabs and Jews live in reconciliation.

In fact, throughout his life, Saada kept in touch with his friend, Yasser Arafat, and shared the love of Jesus with him. Saada testified that four months before Arafat died, he received Christ as his savior! Saada's autobiography is called *Once An Arafat Man*.

Saada points out that God not only loves the Jewish people, but also Palestinian Arabs. Many Christians well remember that God made a covenant with Abraham, but often bypass the covenant God made with Ishmael found in Genesis 17:20—"And as for Ishmael, I have heard you. Behold, I have blessed him, and will make him fruitful, and will multiply him exceedingly. He shall beget twelve princes, and I will make him a great nation."

Many, but not all Arabs are descendants of Ishmael. Other Arab peoples call Abraham their father through his second wife, Ketura. Saada points out that today, if you want to count Ishmaelites, you will arrive at twelve groupings:

- The Saudis (some of whom drifted northward to become the Palestinians)
- The Jordanians
- The Iraqis
- The Kuwaitis
- The Qataris
- The seven sheikdoms of the United Arab Emirates—Dubai, Abu Dhabi, Ajman, Fujairah, Ras al-Khaimah, Sharjah, and Umm al-Qaiwain[36]

Saada is not claiming there is a one-to-one correlation of these twelve groups with the twelve sons of Ishmael long ago, but it is interesting that the number twelve perseveres to this day in Ishmaelite demographics. If you add up the numbers of the Ishmaelites in these nations, plus those in the Gaza Strip and West Bank, there are approximately 58 million, according to Saada.

Genesis 25:13–16 shows the early literal fulfillment of God's promise. Ishmael had twelve sons, who became twelve princes according to their nations. Although God's promise to Abraham regarding Isaac was an eternal covenant, God did not say his covenant with Ishmael was eternal. It could be that God's promise to Ishmael was fulfilled in Ishmael's lifetime.

Jewish-Arab conflict has been in existence since early Bible days. To understand the real conflict, one must understand the Scriptures and history. For the Jewish people, the issue is the land, but more importantly, to be recognized as the Jewish state with Jerusalem as its capital. Jerusalem is the most holy place on earth, as this is where the original temple and the second temple were built. In addition, another temple will soon be built as the Bible prophesied (2 Thessalonians 2:3–4 and Revelation 11:1–2).

To the Arabs, the land is also what they fight for, but the issue is really deeper—it is about rejection. Arabs well know that Abraham was a wealthy man when he sent Hagar (Sarah's handmaiden who bore Abraham's first

---

[36] Tass Saada, *Once An Arafat Man: The True Story of How a PLO Sniper Found a New Life* (Tyndale House Publishers, Inc., 2008), 207–208.

son) and Ishmael out of his household. He did not send them away with honor and riches one would expect to be given to one who had been promised that he would be the father of a great nation. Ishmael and Hagar wandered in the desert instead for a brief time, but later returned to Abraham's tents.

This story of Abraham and Ishmael is not only in our Bible, but also in the Qur'an. They have been fighting for *their* nation and *their* land and *their* recognition for millennia. We must trust the sovereignty of God as He was the one who told Abraham to send Hagar and Ishmael away. It was God's plan that the land where Abraham lived was to be given to his son, Isaac—not Ishmael. Ishmael was promised a nation, *but not land* (Genesis 16:10–12).

We may not agree with how the Arabs are negotiating and using terrorism to gain control, but we do need to remember that our God is the God of Abraham, Ishmael, and Isaac. He had a plan for all the peoples who came from Abraham.[37] After forty centuries this population is still trying to get recognition. Ishmael got pushed out of the camp of his father, Abraham—and his descendants today are still trying to get back in.[38] They truly do not understand the land covenant God made with Isaac, the son of Abraham's legitimate wife. They are fighting to gain land (Israel) that God did not promise to them (Ishmael).

Although there is a constant struggle between the descendants of Isaac and the descendants of Ishmael, in the future, God will bless both nations. It is interesting to note how Isaiah 19 closes: "In that day Israel will be one of three with Egypt and Assyria—a blessing in the midst of the land, whom the LORD of hosts shall bless, saying, 'Blessed is Egypt My people, and Assyria the work of My hands, and Israel My inheritance.'" God's plan to bless both Isaac and Ishmael will be played out in the future—during the thousand-year reign of Christ.

For years it has been thought that a two-state solution was the answer to the disputed land of Israel. There has been talk more recently of a one-state solution.

---

[37] Tass Saada, *Once An Arafat Man: The True Story of How a PLO Sniper Found a New Life* (Tyndale House Publishers, Inc., 2008), 211.
[38] Ibid, 212.

The Two-State Solution Examined

It does not appear likely that a two-state solution will come to pass any time soon. However, to consider the history of peace negotiations between Israel and the Palestinians, one may scratch one's head and wonder why the two-state solution keeps finding its way to the negotiation table.

During Benjamin Netanyahu's campaign for the 2015 elections, he said there would be no two-state solution and no Palestinian state under him because the implementation of that vision is not relevant right now. He said that in response to the attacks Israel has experienced as a result of giving the Gaza Strip to the Palestinians. They have not proven to be friendly neighbors who kept their word about trading land for peace. Netanyahu and most Israelis agree that the Palestinians should have their own state, but there must be a deal in which, if given that state, they would be held accountable for living in peace as neighbors.

Prime Minister Benjamin Netanyahu gave an address during the Knesset session dedicated to Jerusalem Day in May 2017, in which he said, among other things, "The Temple Mount and the Western Wall will forever remain under Israeli sovereignty. The correction of a historical injustice that was achieved by the heroism of our fighters 50 years ago will stand forever." Yet the Israeli Knesset are not united on this topic.

A two-state solution cannot be worked out right now because the Palestinian president will not accept Israel as a Jewish state and has made a pact with Hamas that calls for the destruction of Israel. As then U.S. House Speaker John Boehner put it, "How do you have a two-state solution when you don't have a partner in that solution, when you don't have a partner for peace, when the other state has vowed to wipe you off the face of the Earth?" [39]

---

[39] "Boehner: Obama administration's 'animosity' toward Netanyahu 'reprehensible,'" *The Jerusalem Post*, March 29, 2015, http://www.jpost.com/Israel-News/Boehner-describes-Obama-administrations-animosity-towards-Netanyahu-as-reprehensible-395506.

The One-State Solution Examined

Caroline Glick is a US-born Israeli journalist, newspaper editor, and writer. She moved to Israel shortly after her university studies. Glick is the deputy managing editor of *The Jerusalem Post*. In her well-documented book, *The Israeli Solution*, she presents a lengthy explanation in favor of a one-state solution, along with anticipated responses from worldwide powers. She makes the following observation regarding Israel's right to exist as the Jewish state:

> It is easy to understand why the Palestinians believe it is imperative that they deny Jewish history. If they acknowledge the validity of the region's Jewish roots, they will be forced to recognize that the Jews rather than the Palestinian Arabs are the indigenous people of the land. This state of affairs is so obvious that even the PLO has admitted it.[40]

In January 2011, Al Jazeera and *The Guardian* published what they referred to as "the Palestine Papers." The papers, leaked to Al Jazeera, were in large part written by the Palestinian Negotiations Support Unit, which is the Palestinian Authority department responsible for packaging and marketing the Palestinians' negotiating positions. The leaked papers included thousands of documents.

One of the leaked documents was titled "Strategy and Talking Points for Responding to the Precondition of Recognizing Israel as a 'Jewish State.'" In the document, the NSU explained that Palestinian negotiators must never recognize Israel's right to exist as the Jewish state. It instructed Palestinian negotiators to limit their recognition to Israel's Jewish identity:

> Recognizing Israel as a "Jewish state," particularly in advance of agreeing to the final border between Israel and Palestine, could also strengthen Israel's claims of sovereignty

---

[40] Caroline B. Glick, *The Israeli Solution: A One-State Plan for Peace in the Middle East*, (New York: Crown Forum, 2014), 183.

over all of Historic Palestine, including the OPT [Occupied Palestinian Territory]. Recognizing the Jewish state implies recognition of a Jewish people and recognition of its right to self-determination. Those who assert this right also assert that the territory historically associated with this right of self-determination (i.e., the self-determination unit) is all of Historic Palestine. Therefore, recognition of the Jewish people and their right of self-determination may lend credence to the Jewish people's claim to all of Historic Palestine.

So for the Palestinians, even the most basic recognition of reality—that Israel is a Jewish state—threatens their entire edifice of lies.[41]

Even though the West Bank is the Biblical heartland for the Jews and the strategic heartland for Israel, the Israelis would be willing to give it over in a heartbeat if it would mean one thing. What do you think that *one thing* would be? Peace. However, Israel would be foolish to agree to any "land for peace" agreement, as history has proven that the Palestinians are not interested in peace, given the use of the Gaza Strip by the terrorist group Hamas. They have not proven to be friendly neighbors and continue to call for the destruction of Israel. How could Israel expect any lasting peace with those who vow Israel's annihilation?

Palestinians have never been open to land-for-peace offers. I do not believe the Palestinians will ever agree to any proposal that includes provision for recognition of a Jewish state. If the Palestinians were given the land, Israel would still have valid concerns that there would be no peace, based on past experience.

Sandra Teplinsky states, "Let us not be naïve; history shows that ideology, not occupation, is the primary cause of today's terror. Until Yahweh dramatically intervenes (and I believe He will), we ought not to expect

[41] Caroline B. Glick, *The Israeli Solution: A One-State Plan for Peace in the Middle East.* (New York: Crown Forum, 2014), 183–184.

things to change very much for very long."[42] I agree with Teplinsky's statement—there will be no real peace in Israel or between the Palestinians and the Jewish people until the Prince of Peace returns. Perhaps the solution is no solution. Perhaps to leave things as they are, even as volatile as they may be, is the best solution.

Meanwhile, how shall we respond?

Will you stand with Israel as it continues to struggle for its right to exist? Will you stand with Israel as it seeks to defend itself from terrorism?

I hope you will now be prepared to share the truth with others when you are asked:

- What about the "occupation?"
- What about the refugees?
- Why won't Israel allow a Palestinian state?

The Middle East issues are not simple. When history is properly understood, one gains a better grasp of what Israel faces today and why it reacts the way it does. Also, one can better understand the anger of the Palestinians and their leaders' poor decisions in refusing these peace plans generation after generation—rejecting offer after offer and embracing terrorism instead.

---

[42] Sandra Teplinsky, *Why Care About Israel?: How the Jewish Nation Is the Key to Unleashing God's Blessings in the 21st Century.* (Grand Rapids, Mich.: Chosen Books, 2004), 201.

PART FOUR

Spiritual Israel

CHAPTER 9

Distortion Reigns

For almost two thousand years, many denominations making up "the church" have maintained that because the Jews rejected Jesus as their Messiah and crucified Him, that God is finished with the Jewish people and Israel. They use the fact that God poured out His wrath on Jerusalem in AD 70 when their temple was destroyed and much of Israel was exiled as proof of God's rejection. Furthermore, these same denominations today believe that because God has rejected Israel, there is no place in God's plan for the Jewish people; they have become an apartheid nation; and God has transferred the promises and blessing He reserved for them to the church.

Replacement Theology

Also called *Supersessionism* or *Fulfillment Theology*, *replacement theology* is a Christian theological view on the current status of the Church in relation to the Jewish people, Judaism and the State of Israel, claiming that the Church has replaced national Israel in relation to the promises of God.

Unfortunately, many churches today are in the replacement theology camp, and the numbers seem to be growing. I called Dr. Michael Brown's radio talk show, *Line of Fire*,[43] to ask if he knew of a statistic indicating what percentage of churches in America align with replacement theology. He

---

[43] Brown, Dr. Michael, radio talk show *Line of Fire*, May 19, 2017.

said there is no way to come up with that statistic with tens of thousands of individual churches and denominations. However, he said that it is growing again in the Church and teaching replacement theology has, in the past, led to anti-Semitism. This is a concern. This ignorance about Israel has been passed on to us historically and it goes back to a severing of our Jewish roots.

Yet the beginnings of the Church were Jewish. The Church was formed in Judea by Jews who met the Jewish Messiah, Yeshua (Jesus Christ). They were the first to accept Him as the Savior promised through their own Hebrew Scriptures.

Satan hates the Jewish people with a passion. He hates Christians also. ("Be sober, be vigilant; because your adversary the devil walks about like a roaring lion, seeking whom he may devour." 1 Peter 5:8) But Satan hates Jews because God gave them the Bible and it was through Abraham's seed that Messiah came. This hatred goes back to the beginning of time. God outlined His plan of redemption through them and promised there would always be a remnant of Jews in the world. Satan hates Jews because they are God's chosen people – the apple of His eye (Zechariah 2:8) and He loves them with an everlasting love.

When one recognizes Satan's goal—to defeat God's redemptive purposes for the world, using Israel as His ve-hicle—one can see his actions as the root of replacement theology. God chose Israel to complete His plan. If Satan can attack that plan and turn it around, then he feels he has a chance to become God.

> God's chosen people were first called *Hebrew* from their word *'ibrî*, which meant something like *one from beyond the river*, that is, the Jordan. After the tribes were exiled during the Babylonian captivity they were named *Jews*, identifying them as having come from Judah.

When God became angry over Israel's unbelief in Messiah, it was prophesied that the temple would be destroyed. It was a consequence of Israel's disbelief and as a result, God scattered His people. Does that mean God is finished with Israel? To the contrary—He also promised to regather them and is doing that today. Even when Israel was scattered, God told them they would be regathered. It is no coincidence that "Israel became a nation in a day" on May 14, 1948. The prophecy of Isaiah 66:7–8 was fulfilled:

Before she goes into labor, she gives birth; before the pains come upon her, she delivers a son. Who has ever heard of such things? Who has ever seen things like this? Can a country be born in a day or a nation be brought forth in a moment? (NIV)

The woman giving birth before going into labor represents Israel. This accurately describes what happened on May 14, 1948, when the Jews declared independence for Israel as a united and sovereign nation for the first time in 2,900 years. Only hours prior to this, the United Nations mandate expired, ending British control of the land. During a twenty-four–hour period, the British Mandate ended and Israel had declared its independence. Its independence was acknowledged by the United States and other nations. Modern Israel was literally born in a single day!

Does this sound like God is finished with Israel? Not at all. God promised He would bring the Jewish people back to Israel, although in unbelief. It is impossible for God to renege on a promise (Numbers 23:19). Then He says they will go through more trials while living in the land. God will act out miracles on their behalf and in the last days, their unbelief will turn to belief (Romans 11:26).

God is still working out His plan. To say that God is finished with Israel makes no sense. It would be calling God a liar. It is impossible for God to lie (Titus 1:2, Hebrews 6:18).

When the Church began, it was wholly Jewish. It wasn't until Peter preached in Caesarea to Cornelius that Gentiles even entered the Church (Acts 10). Gentiles became part of the fulfilled Jewish movement. Our Christian roots are Jewish. Mankind has tried to ignore this point and through the ages has changed what God intended the Church to look like. When someone comes to believe in Messiah, it is a Jewish Messiah whom we serve. We are grafted into Jewish roots, as Paul explains in Romans 11 (see Chapter 4, "The Relationship between Jews and Gentiles").

Many say that because the Jews rejected Jesus, that God has rejected them. In the same verses that explain their rejection, Scripture is clear that the Jews have not been rejected by God.

> I say then, have they [the Jews] stumbled that they should
> fall? Certainly not! But through their fall, to provoke them
> to jealousy, salvation has come to the Gentiles. (Romans
> 11:11)

This Scripture gives a definitive answer to the question: "Has God rejected His people?" We see an emphatic NO! The Scripture teaches that the
Jews have not been rejected by God because of their unbelief. This is confirmed in many other scriptures.

> What advantage then has the Jew, or what is the profit
> of circumcision? Much in every way! Chiefly because to
> them were committed the oracles of God. For what if some
> did not believe? Will their unbelief make the faithfulness
> of God without effect? Certainly not! Indeed, let God be
> true ... (Romans 3:1–4a)

Paul confirms that Jesus has not nullified God's faithfulness to the
promises He made to the Jewish people. In addition, God entrusted the
Jewish people with His gospel—which was originally given to Abraham; he
was saved by *faith* in God (Romans 4:3). God's calling to the Jews is irrevocable (Romans 11:29). He made wonderful promises to the Jewish people
and to their descendants, the people of Israel, and God must keep those
promises to validate His own righteousness. Those promises and all the gifts
mentioned in Romans 9:4–5 are irrevocable because God cannot deny his
own eternal nature as a faithful fulfiller of promises.

He called the Jews to be a people dedicated to Himself, a holy nation
(Exodus 19:6), and a light to the Gentiles (Isaiah 42:6, 49:6). When one studies Romans Chapters 9–11 and considers the above verses, it becomes evident
that any Christian theology which teaches that God no longer loves the

Jews, or that the Jewish people will not receive all the good things God has promised them, contradicts the express teaching of the New Testament.[44]

Although God has not changed His eternal promise to the Jewish people, there is a consequence to the Jews for rejecting Messiah. God is disciplining them for that rejection today. As a result God has blinded some of them temporarily. God has scattered the people after the rejection of Messiah. They are still scattered, but being regathered. About the discipline and the promise, read Jeremiah 30:11.

> "For I am with you," says the LORD, "to save you; Though I make a full end of all the nations where I have scattered you, yet I will not make a complete end of you. But I will correct you in justice, and will not let you go altogether unpunished."

God still loves the Jewish people today and continues with His original plan for them. It is an everlasting plan. It has not been transferred to the Church or anyone else, although the Church receives the blessing of salvation and is not loved less than Israel.

Unfortunately, Christian colleges and universities have faculty members who are speaking out against Israel and subscribe to replacement theology. They teach that the Palestinians have the right to the land that God decreed to the Jewish people. They have not considered the full counsel of God in His Word. They have not considered the everlasting and unconditional covenant made to Abraham.

Christian Palestinianism

In his book, *For Zion's Sake*, Dr. Paul Wilkinson defines "Christian Palestinianism" by comparing it to "Christian Zionism."

---

[44] David H. Stern, *Jewish New Testament Commentary: A Companion Volume to the Jewish New Testament* (Clarksville, Md.: Jewish New Testament Publications, 1992) 424, ref. Romans 11:28–29.

Christian Palestinianism is an inverted mirror image of Christian Zionism. All the basic elements of a Christian Zionist eschatology are reversed, so that:

- The Bible is seen to be Christian, not Jewish.
- The land of the Bible is Palestine—not Israel.
- The son of God is a Palestinian (Jesus was the first Palestinian martyr)—not a Jew.
- The Holocaust is resented—not remembered.
- 1948 is a catastrophe—not a miracle.
- The Jewish people are illegal occupiers—not rightful owners.
- The State of Israel is illegitimate—not the fulfillment of prophecy.
- Biblical prophecy is a moral manifesto—not a signpost to the Second Coming.[45]

If you think this is not a big deal, look at this partial list representing followers of Christian Palestinianism who attended the Christ at the Checkpoint Conference in Bethlehem in 2012 and propagated the Christian Palestinian lies:

- Stephen Sizer, incumbent of the Anglican parish of Christ Church, in Surry, England
- Gary Burge, Ph.D., New Testament professor at Wheaton College, Illinois
- Tony Campolo, pastor and one of the most influential leaders in the Evangelical left in the United States, who characterizes Christian Zionism as "theology that legitimizes oppression"
- John Ortberg, Christian author, speaker and senior pastor of Menlo Park Presbyterian Church, Menlo Park, California
- World Vision

---

[45] Paul R. Wilkinson, *For Zion's Sake: Christian Zionism and the Role of John Nelson Darby* (Nottingham, England: Paternoster, 2007), 65.

- World Council of Churches, with 345 member churches, who represent more than half a billion Christians around the world
- World Evangelical Alliance, a global organization of churches, which claims to represent 600 million evangelicals around the world

Author Olivier Melnick has written, "Christian Palestinianism is a distorted view of God's Word hiding a political agenda behind a reformed theology, resulting in a presentation of Christian Zionism as heretical."[47] God began His written Word to us by telling us at the beginning that He

> ...people will believe a big lie sooner than a little one; and if you repeat it frequently enough people will sooner or later believe it.
> —excerpt from a U.S. Office of Strategic Services report titled *A Psychological Analysis of Adolph Hitler His Life and Legend*[46]

made an eternal covenant with Abraham and His descendants, that they were His chosen people and that He gave them a land designated for them. However, today's culture is thirsty for social justice and tolerance and has turned many "Evangelicals" toward Christian Palestinianism, ignoring the clear Word of God.

It is appalling that Christian Palestinians are naming Jesus as the "first Palestinian" just because He was born in Bethlehem, which is under the Palestinian Authority today. Then, developing this thought, they insist that God favors the Palestinian people and not the Jewish people. They condemn Zionists for their support of Israel.

God made an everlasting covenant with Abraham and *his* descendants through Isaac—the Hebrews—later referred to as the Jews ... never with Palestinians. The Scripture says that the covenant continues throughout their generations for an everlasting covenant (Genesis 15:18, 17:7–13, 28:4,

---

[46] "Hitler as His Associates Know Him," in *A Psychological Analysis of Adolph Hitler His Life and Legend*, Walter C. Langer, (Washington, D.C.: Office of Strategic Services), The Nizkor Project, http://www.nizkor.org/hweb/people/h/hitler-adolf/oss-papers/text/oss-profile-03-02.html, accessed April 13, 2017.

[47] Olivier Melnick, "The Six Dangers of Christian Palestinianism," Fight the New Antisemitism, March 25, 2015, http://www.newantisemitism.com/antisemitism/the-six-dangers-of-christian-palestinianism.

13, Leviticus 26:45, Acts 7:5, and others) To say that God's favor and promises are now with the Palestinians makes God a liar because He would have broken the Abrahamic Covenant. This is entirely untrue and so against the nature of God (see Chapter 3, "Four Covenants Woven Together").

I believe we are in the end times, and that the closer we get to the end, the more we will see Israel as the central point of division, even among Christians. Our best weapon of defense is to *know* the Word of God inside and out and not be prone to deception.

To better understand world conflicts today, we must understand God's Word.

I encourage you to study, like you have never studied before, and be like the wise men in the court of Xerxes (Esther 1:13) and the men from the tribe of Issachar (1 Chronicles 12:32), who had an understanding of the times.

Distortions fuel conflict and expose Israel to potential damage.

CHAPTER 10

Anti-Semitism Can Lead to Aliyah

God never allows anything to happen without purpose. Jewish people may ask, "Why does it appear the entire world is against us?" Throughout the world, anti-Semitism is consistent with Bible prophecy. From the beginning of time, God has loved His chosen people and has had a plan to use them to accomplish His purposes as He continues to do to this day. Yet, anti-Semitism—hostility to or prejudice against the Jewish people—has been a part of history for millennia. Is this part of God's plan?

The term *anti-Semitism* was coined in the late nineteenth century in Germany; it simply meant *Jew-hatred*. Anti-Semitism was defined in 2005 in a U.S. governmental report as "hatred toward Jews—individually and as a group—that can be attributed to the Jewish religion and/or ethnicity."[48]

Those involved in anti-Semitism are deceived and do not study the Bible with the Jewish people in mind, if they read it at all. But instead, they read the Scripture out of context. Their conclusion is not to care about Israel or the Jewish people. Today this, unfortunately, even applies to many Christian church leaders. Many believe Israel does not have the right to exist today.

> All racism is evil, but there is something different and even more insidious about antisemitism.
> —Mitch Glaser,
> Chosen People Ministries

If they thought through their arguments scripturally, they would see that if

---

[48] "Report on Global Anti-Semitism", U.S. State Department, 5 January 2005.

there was no Israel today, there would be no second coming of Jesus—Jesus will return to the city of Jerusalem—it must be here when He comes.

Anti-Semitism Around the World

In a personal letter to the Song For Israel ministry from the executive director of International Christian Embassy Jerusalem, Dr. Jürgen Buhler wrote:

> Israel is facing again a new wave of hatred from the world, which is beyond any logical comprehension. The call to boycott, divest and sanction Israel (BDS) is hitting Israel in unprecedented strength. The French cellphone giant Orange considered stopping its many years long operation in Israel. At the same time a large investment fund in Norway is removing any Israeli investments from its fund which has connection to settlements in Judea and Samaria. Finally, the European Union is planning to mark all products from Israel as illegal if the company has any relationship to any settlements.
>
> It not only reminds us of what happened in Nazi Germany some seventy years ago, when German citizens were told not to buy from Jews, but it also demonstrates an unacceptable double standard as disproportionate sanctions are applied to Israel when other countries are committing far worse human rights abuses. Within the body of the United Nations it cannot even be called double standard anymore. The human rights council of the UN is headed today by states like Algeria, China, Cuba, Ethiopia, Kazakhstan, the Maldives, Qatar, Russia, Saudi Arabia and Venezuela. The moral standards of these nations are known. They rubber stamp their own countries' faults but are united to condemn Israel. They say "the world will not tolerate the injustice caused by Israel anymore."

In Chapter 2 of this book, you will find a long (but partial) list of anti-Semitic acts that have been committed throughout history.

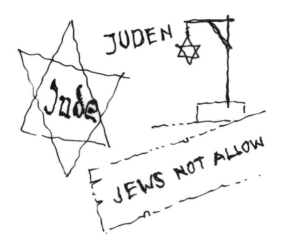

American Anti-Semitism

America has been, for the most part, friendly toward the Jewish people. They have been welcomed when they immigrated from other parts of the world; they have become prosperous business owners and have been able to freely worship in their synagogues.

However, in some instances, hatred of the Jewish people was a cultural value imported to the United States from Europe. Although Jewish Americans felt more comfortable and secure than ever before, there has still been a thread of anti-Semitism throughout our history.

In recent years we have seen a rise in anti-Semitism in America. There have been an alarming number of anti-Israel and anti-Zionist activities on our college and university campuses. I attended one such event at Cal State Fullerton, where Palestinians For Justice held their first meeting, showed a slanted documentary called *Five Broken Cameras,* and led a distorted discussion on hatred toward Israel.

Although a few of those pro-Israel people who attended with me gave their best shot at discrediting the lies that were being presented, neither the leaders nor those in the audience were willing to listen. This is happening on campuses around our nation and is shaping young minds. View this video interviewing Jewish students on American campuses to better understand what they are facing: https://www.youtube.com/watch?v=gAyFlByb64M.

Mitch Glaser of Chosen People Ministries explains Jewish immigration from Europe to America:

> From the late 19th into the early 20th century, approximately 3 million Jewish people fled persecution in Europe [heading] for the United States—which was known as the Goldina Medina, or "Golden Land." The 1986 animated film *An American Tail* depicts this journey, as Fievel Mousekewitz, a Jewish mouse, and his family flee from ferocious cats in Russia. These cats represent the Cossacks who carried out pogroms, or violent riots, against Jewish villages in Russia and Eastern Europe. The Mousekewitz family believed that living in America would alleviate their problems, but when they arrived, they discovered that cats live here too.
>
> Even so, for the most part, America has treated the Jewish community better than any other nation in history. George Washington established a strong relationship between the United States and its Jewish citizens. Since the first American Colonies, the United States has provided a place where the Jewish people have flourished ... [hence, the reason we have experienced God's blessing in America.]
>
> Yet while America remains the Goldina Medina, the existence of anti-Semitism must not be overlooked. Just as the Mousekewitz family discovered "cats" in America, Jewish immigrants to the United States have faced notable instances of prejudice.[49]

---

[49] Mitch Glaser, "A Painful Past," Chosen People Ministries Newsletter, June 2013, 5, https://www.chosenpeople.com/site/newsletters/1306NL.pdf

Anti-Semitism in America didn't begin with World War II. It has been here for hundreds of years. Chosen People Ministries published the following notable instances of American Anti-Semitism:

- 1862: General Grant expelled the Jewish people from Tennessee, Kentucky, and Mississippi. Fortunately, President Lincoln quickly revoked this order.
- 1913: A young Jewish man named Leo Frank moved from Brooklyn to work as an engineer and superintendent in Atlanta. In April 1913, Frank faced false accusations of strangling a thirteen-year-old girl at the factory. His trial portrayed Frank as part of the northern Jewish aristocracy who perpetually took advantage of the vulnerable and underprivileged. An angry mob abducted Frank, hung him, and then beat his body into disfigurement.
- 1915: Crowds celebrated Frank's conviction and used his caricature as a means of calling for reestablishment of Ku Klux Klan in 1915. The Jewish community founded the Anti-Defamation League to fight anti-Semitism.
- 1918: Henry Ford acquired the weekly newspaper *The Dearborn Independent*, in which he published regular anti-Semitic rants. For example, he accused Jewish people of instigating World War I for profit. He blamed "German-Jewish bankers" for the war and believed that "the Jew is a threat." Ford also perpetuated a false anti-Semitic publication called *The Protocols of the Elders of Zion*, which outlined a Jewish plan for world domination. The document was later proved a hoax.
- 1930: Father Coughlin, a Catholic priest, became a prominent voice for anti-Semitic hatred. He created a weekly radio program with an audience as large as 12 million, and his broadcasts accused Jewish bankers of causing both the Depression and the Russian Revolution. He also publicly sympathized with Nazi Germany and Hitler's policies.

- Present: Instances of anti-Semitism in America declined in the aftermath of World War II though a few fringe groups still deny the Holocaust, claiming it was a hoax and a Jewish conspiracy.[50]

Unfortunately, one can continue to find acts of American anti-Semitism in the local news on a regular basis.

For many decades, Evangelical support for Israel seemed rock solid. Today, however, many younger Christians in Western churches are hesitant to give Israel the same unconditional support which their parents did. Studies of Palestinian suffering, rather than the struggles and triumphs of Israel, have attracted the sympathy of young Evangelicals.[51]

Today's anti-Semitism has many flavors:

Boycotts, Divestments, and Sanctions (BDS Movement)

Israel faces a new onslaught of hatred from around the world. With each wave, we scratch our heads and ask, "Why is this happening to the Jewish people?" The newest form of anti-Semitism in Israel is the call to boycott, divest, and sanction. According to the Anti-Defamation League, proponents of BDS also called for pressure on governments "to impose broad boycotts and implement divestment initiatives against Israel." A key element of the BDS campaign is the specific rejection of a two-state solution to the conflict. "The campaign was endorsed by pro-Palestinian organizations in Europe and the United States and the call for BDS against Israel has since become a key tactic within the global effort to delegitimize and isolate Israel."[52]

As of 2015, the European Union is planning to mark all products from Israel as illegal if a company has *any* relationship to any settlements (communities in "disputed" territories).

---

[50] Mitch Glaser, "A Painful Past," *Chosen People Ministries Newsletter*, June 2013, 2–3, https://www.chosenpeople.com/site/newsletters/1306NL.pdf
[51] Jürgen Buhler, "Jesus and the Palestinians," *Word From Jerusalem*, May 2014, 6–9
[52] "BDS: The Global Campaign to Delegitimize Israel," Anti-Defamation League, accessed April 26, 2017, https://www.adl.org/education/resources/backgrounders/bds-the-global-campaign-to-delegitimize-israel-0.

Hate Speech

The first step in terrorism is hate speech, that is, speech that attacks a person or group based on attributes such as gender, ethnic origin, religion, race, disability, or sexual orientation. It typically leads to violence and terror attacks.

Barnes & Noble Inc. and the Anti-Defamation League launched a collaborative campaign, Close the Book on Hate, in September 2000. The initiative was designed to help break the cycle of learned intolerance through one of the best forms of education—reading. This campaign empowers children and their parents, caregivers, teachers, and civic leaders with the resources and programs they need to help end prejudice and discrimination in America. The campaign includes the prominent display of a new section of specially selected anti-bias books in Barnes & Noble stores across the country and in-store educational programs and events.

> You don't need a knife, a gun or a truck to inflict damage on the population, words can be as damaging!

Social Media Anti-Semitism

The World Jewish Congress (WJC) reports that in 2016 there were 382,000 anti-Semitic posts found online—that translates to one post every 83 seconds. 31,000 posts call for violence against Jews. According to a YouTube from the WJC called *The Rise of Anti-Semitism in Social Media: Summary of 2016,* the most common posts are to gas, burn or kill Jews. These social media platforms where anti-Semitic posts are found include:

63% Twitter

11% Facebook

6% Instagram

2% You Tube

When you see an anti-Semitic post, get involved and use these opportunities to respond with lovingkindness and truth.

Silence

Anti-Semitism can also be seen by Americans who are silent in the face of opposition to the Jewish people. As Christians, we are to bless the Jewish people (Genesis 12:3), which means when we see others speaking out against the Jews, we are not to remain silent. We are to join hands with our Jewish neighbors and stand *with* them. Our silence can be just as destructive as hate speech.

Delegitimization

The State of Israel bears the brunt of many arguments regarding legitimacy. Israel is often labeled as a "settler state" or "colonizer of people." Many claim Israel is an "apartheid state" (see Chapter 7). Israel has been a legitimate member of the United Nations since May 11, 1949, yet many UN member states do not recognize Israel as a legitimate government. As Barry Shaw wrote in *The Jerusalem Post:*

> When U.S. Secretary of State John Kerry said it was a "mistake" for Israel to demand recognition as the Jewish state, it showed how deeply the language of delegitimization has been adopted by even the most ardent of Israel supporters....
>
> We increasingly see well-intentioned, powerful and influential people, who have the close attention of the media, make misplaced statements that feed into the adoption of a viewpoint that Israel has no legitimate right to be where it is. The misuse of language and deed is an indicator not only of the general public's views, it also displays how pro-Israel influential voices are chasing a narrative that is driven by the Palestinian side of the conflict.[53]

---

[53] Barry Shaw, "Original thinking: When Israel supporters use the language of delegitimization," *The Jerusalem Post*, April 7, 2014, http://www.jpost.com/printarticle.aspx?id=347822

Sadly, many of Israel's historic sites have been stripped of their ancient ties to Jewish history by organizations such as the United Nations Educational, Scientific and Cultural Organization (UNESCO). Some of these sites include the Temple Mount and the Cave of the Patriarchs (where Abraham, Sarah, Isaac, Rebecca, Jacob and Leah were buried). In 2017 UNESCO voted to deny Jerusalem's right to be Israel's capital.

The New Anti-Semitism

Anti-Semitism continues today in a new sophisticated form called "anti-Zionism" which refuses to accept the Jewish people's right to live in their own land. They denounce those who teach that the Bible's promises concerning the land of Israel are being fulfilled today. They claim that the Abrahamic Covenant does not apply to a particular ethnic group, but rather to the Church of Jesus Christ—the "true Israel." They believe that the land promised specifically to Israel in the Old Testament was fulfilled under Joshua. That is not true as neither Joshua, nor anyone since, has been able to conquer all the land that is delineated in the Abrahamic Covenant.

In addition, these anti-Zionists claim that the present secular State of Israel is not an authentic or prophetic realization of the messianic kingdom of Jesus Christ. Furthermore, a day should not be anticipated in which Christ's kingdom will manifest Jewish distinctives, whether by its location, by its constituency, or by its ceremonial institutions and practices. These views are rooted in replacement theology, as discussed in Chapter 9.

Apartheid Week

Colleges and universities all over America are promoting annual anti-Israel conferences under the banner of "Israeli Apartheid Week." Their goal is to indoctrinate people about Israel's ongoing settler-colonial project and apartheid policies over the Palestinian people. It is their hope that these demonstrations will promote a powerful contribution to the Palestinian struggle for freedom and justice. Some also claim that Israel should be destroyed.

Campus Intifadas

The word *intifada* is Arabic for "tremor" or "shuddering" and has come to mean "uprising," "rebellion," or "resistance" in the modern context of the Palestinian struggle against Israel. Campus intifadas are taking place on various major American university campuses with the majority of them occurring on the West Coast.

Students for Justice in Palestine (SJP), is an offshoot of the Muslim Student Association (established by the Muslim Brotherhood) who are active in 189 colleges and universities across America. In my area of Southern California, I have heard about many campus intifadas occurring at University of California, Irvine (UCI). When a pro-Israel student group meets on campus, there have been many occasions where they have met resistance. To view one such occasion, please visit https://www.youtube.com/watch?v=eEmq1j0mdFk to watch a video of Anti-Zionist students disrupting a Students Supporting Israel event at UCI.

Waves of *Aliyah*—Jewish People Returning to Israel

Scripture points out that God uses all things to work together for good to accomplish His purposes (Romans 8:28). He seems to be using anti-Semitism in many nations to move the Jewish people back into the land of Israel. We can trace throughout history where the Jewish people have been exiled or expelled—starting back with the destruction of Israel in AD 70. They have been scattered all over the globe and are referred to as the diaspora.

Many Scriptures refer to a day when the Jewish people will return to the land of their ancestors:

- He [God] will set up a banner for the nations, and will assemble the outcasts of Israel, and gather together the dispersed of Judah from the four corners of the earth. (Isaiah 11:12)
- "Fear not, for I am with you; I will bring your descendants from the east, and gather you from the west; I will say to the north, 'Give them up!' and to the south, 'Do Not keep them back!' Bring My sons

from afar, and My daughters from the ends of the earth." (Isaiah 43:5–6)

- "I will bring them back into their land which I gave to their fathers." (Jeremiah 16:15)
- "But I will gather the remnant of My flock out of all the countries where I have driven them, and bring them back to their folds; and they shall be fruitful and increase." (Jeremiah 23:3)
- "'Therefore do not fear, O My servant Jacob,' says the LORD, 'Nor be dismayed, O Israel; For behold, I will save you from afar, and your seed from the land of their captivity. Jacob [Israel] shall return, have rest and be quiet, and no one shall make him afraid. For I am with you,' says the LORD, 'to save you; though I will make a full end of all the nations where I have scattered you …'" (Jeremiah 30:10–11)
- "For I [God] will take you [Israel] from among the nations, gather you out of all countries, and bring you into your own land." (Ezekiel 36:24)

In the land of Israel, Jews have always maintained a presence down through the centuries. However, it was during the late 1800s that increasing numbers of Jews, seeking refuge from anti-Semitism and inspired by Zionist ideology, returned to what was then called Palestine. These early pioneers drained swamps, reclaimed wastelands, forested bare hillsides, founded agricultural settlements and revived the Hebrew language for everyday use. The return of the Jewish people to Palestine, restored later to its previous name, Israel, seemed to come in waves.

The following is a list of waves of *Aliyah* to Israel compiled by the International Christian Embassy Jerusalem on their website:

The First Aliyah (1882–1903)—This Aliyah followed pogroms in Russia in 1881–1882, with most of the 35,000 immigrants coming from Eastern Europe, Imperial Russia, and what was later to be the Soviet Union.

The Second Aliyah (1904–1914)—In the wake of pogroms in Czarist Russia, 40,000 young people, inspired by socialist ideals, settled in Palestine.

The Third Aliyah (1919–1923)—This Aliyah was a continuation of the Second Aliyah that was interrupted by World War I and was triggered by the October Revolution in Russia and the pogroms in Poland and Hungary.

The Fourth Aliyah (1924–1929)—The Fourth Aliyah was a direct result of the anti-Jewish policies in Poland and stiff immigration quotas in America.

The Fifth Aliyah (1929–1939)—This Aliyah was a result of the Nazi accession to power in Germany (1933).

Aliyah During World War II and Its Aftermath (1939–1948)—Efforts were focused on rescuing the Jews from Nazi occupied Europe. The *Yishuv* (Jewish community in Palestine prior to the declaration of the State of Israel), Jewish partisans, and Zionist youth movements cooperated in establishing the *Beriah* (escape) organization, which assisted 200,000 European Jews with their immigration to Palestine.

Exodus of 1947 (1945–1947)—During this period, the number of immigrants, legal and illegal alike, was 480,000—90 percent of them from Europe.

Mass Immigration After 1948—When the State of Israel was proclaimed May 14, 1948, the Proclamation of the State of Israel stated: "The State of Israel will be open for Jewish immigration and the ingathering of the Exiles; it will foster the development of the country for all of its inhabitants; it will be based on freedom, justice and peace envisioned by the prophets of Israel ..."

Mass immigration from the former Soviet Union—(1989 to the end of 2010)—more than one million Jewish people from the former Soviet Union have made their home in Israel. There are another million Jews still in the former Soviet Union, and there are 800,000 in Germany, the USA, and Canada.[54]

Reestablished as the national homeland of the Jewish people, Israel has a population that includes Jews of every geographic, ethnic, and religious identity. Seventy-five percent of Israelis are Jewish.[55]

The Jewish people have been returning to the land God promised them just as Scripture said they would. It appears that persecution of Jews around the world has played a part in driving the Jewish people home.

---

[54] "Waves of Aliyah," International Christian Embassy Jerusalem website, accessed April 14, 2017. https://int.icej.org/aid/defining-aliyah.

[55] "Diversity," StandWithUs, accessed April 14, 2017, http://standwithus.com/qr/diversity.html.

How We Can Combat Anti-Semitism

When anti-Semitism erupts in one way or another in the community in which you live, stand against this evil and let your Jewish friends know you stand with them. To do nothing is the same as being their enemy. Loving Israel and the Jewish people should be the most natural thing to do for Christians who understand the biblical mandate of Genesis 12:3—God promises, "I will bless those who bless you [Abram's seed], and I will curse him who curses you."

We can combat anti-Semitism by boldly standing with the Jewish people and Israel. Here are some suggestions:

- When you read magazine or newspaper articles, Facebook posts, blogs, etc., that contain anti-Semitic content, respond by writing to the authors and lovingly share the truth of God's Word and your love for the Jewish people.
- Search for products made in Israel and purchase them. In this way you will combat the boycotts.

In addition to combating anti-Semitism, here are some suggestions to support Israel and the Jewish people:

- Support Messianic Jewish congregations in your area. Visit them on Yom HaShoah, which is a day observed by most congregations in remembrance of the Holocaust.
- Pray for the Jewish people and Israel on a regular basis.
- Consider joining *Song For Israel* in its quest to bless and be supportive of the Jewish people. We offer Israel tours, Feast celebrations, conferences and many other activities in which you can be involved. Support *Song For Israel* financially or donate to our Israel Bomb Shelter campaign. Visit http://songforisrael.org for more information.
- Share the gospel with your Jewish friends by sharing your love for Jesus (use His Hebrew name, Yeshua, when speaking with them).

The Gospel and Anti-Semitism

As followers of the Jewish Messiah, Jesus, we can withstand any encroachment of anti-Semitism in our society and we can demonstrate through our actions that we love the Jewish people. They are often very surprised to find Christians who love them. For example, I have a Jewish friend that I see often at social gatherings. I often greet her with "Shalom!" As a Jewish holiday approaches, I may greet her with the appropriate Hebrew words that correspond with the holiday—for Rosh HaShanah, I would greet her with *"La Shanah Tovah"* (wishes for a good year). She knows that I am a believer in Yeshua, but often tells me, "You are a better Jew than I am!" I am not Jewish, but it is my way of showing her love by greeting her in ways that are dear to her heart. After all, isn't it part of our role as Christians to provoke the Jewish people to jealousy? (Romans 11:7–14)

Our efforts to stand *with* the Jewish people against anti-Semitism whenever and wherever it arises show our Jewish friends support and can only lead to an opportunity to share our beliefs in Messiah with them.

But time is running out. As we look at Biblical prophecies, we see a time-table set before us in which Israel would be regathered in the land. As you now can see, this is occurring before our eyes—and with greater emphasis since Israel became a nation.

Although we are excited to see God's Word being fulfilled in this generation, we may also tremble as Scripture indicates that after Israel returns to her land, there will be large-scale warfare in the Middle East, which will lead up to the great battle—the battle of Armageddon. What will be one of the factors leading up to this battle? I believe anti-Semitism will be the core issue.

Mitch Glaser, president of Chosen People Ministries, explains that anti-Semitism has one cause—Satan:

> Satan has driven a wedge between Israel and the Gospel—so much so that much of the Jewish world is reticent to consider the claims of Jesus as the Messiah. Anti-Semitism has one cause—Satan. Israel plays a crucial role in God's redemptive plan for the world. Therefore, Satan seeks to

thwart God's plan by concentrating his efforts on destroying the Jewish people.

Satan has prompted individuals throughout history to attempt to eradicate the Jewish People. Pharaoh, Antiochus IV, Herod the Great and Adolf Hitler all attempted to thwart God's plan of redemption by killing the Jewish people … These men also failed in their plots, because the nation of Israel is as permanent as the foundation of God's creation (Jeremiah 31:35–37).

Satan's plot became even more sinister when he began using Christianity as the vehicle to persecute the Jewish people. While Satan has failed to destroy the Jewish people, he has not failed to drive a wedge between Israel and the Gospel as a result of the cruelty of those who have gone by the name of "Christian." As a result, much of the Jewish world is reticent to consider the claims of Jesus as the Messiah.

Nothing breaks down two thousand years of prejudice more effectively than love. Somehow we must show Jewish people the difference between Jesus and the Christianity that has hurt them—one person at a time.[56]

While America remains the Golden Land, anti-Semitism is still rooted here and we should not take this lightly. We must stand *with* the Jewish people so that America does not become a persecuting country like so many others where it is not safe for Jewish people to reside.

---

[56] Mitch Glaser, President's Prayer Letter, February 2015, Chosen People Ministries, 241 East 52st Street, New York, NY 10022. Used with permission.

CHAPTER 11

And Finally ... What is the Future for Israel?

God is not finished with Israel or with the Jewish people—God's Word has proven that! But before the thousand-year reign of Christ arrives, much still needs to take place. Following is a brief overview of what Scripture foretells will take place in the last days:

1. Israel will be reestablished as a nation (Isaiah 66:7–8). This occurred in May 1948.
2. The Jewish people will be (are being) regathered in unbelief from the four corners of the earth (Isaiah 11:11–12).
3. All the nations will come against Israel over the issue of the control of Jerusalem (Zechariah 12:2–3).
4. Jerusalem will be occupied by the Jewish people (Zechariah 8:7–8) and, although Israel regained Jerusalem in the 1967 Six-Day War, the world is now questioning this. I believe there will come a day when there will be no question and Israel will occupy and rule Jerusalem.
5. The Antichrist will come to Israel's rescue by guaranteeing them peace by way of a seven-year treaty (contract) and allow them to rebuild their temple and worship in it (Daniel 9:27).
6. In the middle of the seven-year contract, the Antichrist will declare himself to be God (2 Thessalonians 2:3–4).

7. Because the Jewish people will reject the Antichrist, he will come against them in an attempt to annihilate them (Revelation 12:13–17). The nations will gather against Jerusalem (Zechariah 12:9) but the Lord shall appear on the Mount of Olives and fight on their behalf (Zechariah 14:3-4).

8. The Jewish people will finally recognize Jesus, Yeshua, as her Messiah (Zechariah 12:10). They will cry out *"Baruch Haba BaShem Adoni!"* which means "Blessed is he who comes in the name of the Lord" (Matthew 23:39).

9. At this time, all Israel will be saved (Romans 11:26) and Jesus will establish His kingdom.

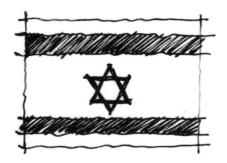

The Jewish people have a very clear and prominent role in Bible prophecy. They have been in the center of God's plan since He chose them and they will continue to be in the center of His plan through the end of time. All that God said He would do, He will do. His promises can be trusted.

The Gentile Believer's Response

Knowing the centrality of Israel in God's plans, one can see why the enemy of Israel (Satan) lurks around to attempt to destroy Israel and, therefore, destroy God's plan. One can see why Israel—a tiny nation in the Middle East—is in the news daily around the world. It is the focus of world attention.

What is our response? We cannot just learn about God's plan for Israel and then sit idly by. God is not looking for fence-sitters. "If we do not get involved, we ourselves may be counted as Israel's enemies." [57] We are called to *stand* with Israel and the Jewish people. In the last days standing with Israel will be a point of division around the world and in our churches. replacement theology has already caused a division in the Church. We must stand for truth and speak it boldly, looking for every venue in which to become involved.

- This book has given you a foundation, but your education must continue. Keep current on the news and get your news from reputable sources (i.e. *The Jerusalem Post, The Times of Israel, International Christian Embassy Jerusalem*).
- Keep up to date with United States' politics and vote for leaders who stand with Israel.
- Purchase Israeli-made goods. Do not participate in boycotts, divestments, or sanctions (BDS) against Israel.
- Become active on social media to discuss issues related to Israel.
- Whenever you are aware of anti-Semitism, stand against it—stand with Israel and the Jewish people! Defend Israel with the truth.
- Teach your children and grandchildren why it is important to love Israel and the Jewish people.
- If you have college students in your home, know where your child's college stands on the issue of Israel and help prepare your son or daughter with the ammunition of truth.
- Visit Israel. Join one of *Song For Israel's* annual tours and experience what the Bible has written about Israel: http://songforisrael.org/indexphp/events-2016-study-tours/
- Get involved and give financially to ministries that support Israel.
- Pray. Scripture tells us we need to "pray for the peace of Jerusalem" in Psalm 122:6. The verse doesn't end there—it goes on to read, "May they prosper who love you." Your own well-being is tied to your prayers for Israel.

---

[57] Sandra Teplinsky. *Why Care About Israel?: How the Jewish Nation Is the Key to Unleashing God's Blessings in the 21st Century*. (Grand Rapids, Mich.: Chosen Books, 2004), 222.

Song FOR ISRAEL

It is my prayer that Christians around the world would embrace the explicit biblical evidence concerning Israel, love and support her, and give God the glory that His promises for Israel still stand! The very fact that God is faithful to Israel is a testimony that His promises will never fail.

> For Zion's sake I will not hold My peace,
> and for Jerusalem's sake I will not rest,
> Until her righteousness goes forth as brightness,
> and her salvation as a lamp that burns.
> (Isaiah 62:1)

APPENDIX

Four Covenants Woven Together

Name	Abrahamic	Mosaic	New Covenant	Davidic
Summary	An everlasting, unconditional covenant God made with Abraham and his descendants promising: *A Seed *A Nation *A Land	A temporary and conditional covenant God made with Moses for the children of Israel, based on obedience. It promised: *Blessings and curses It provided: *A Tabernacle for worship and for God to dwell	An everlasting covenant made to the House of Judah and the House of Israel, promising: *To put His law on their hearts *Forgiveness of sin *That He will be their God and they will be His people The New Testament promises spiritual blessings to Gentiles with faith in Messiah.	This covenant is made with David, providing: *an unending occupancy of David's throne and *promises that the kingdom will be forever.
Scripture References	Genesis 12:1-3, 13:14–16, 15:1-3, 9–12, 17–18, 17:2–11 Romans 4:11-13 Galatians 2:8, 3:29 Hebrews 11:8-10	Exodus 19-24 Deuteronomy 28 Galatians 3:19,24 Hebrews 8:6–7	Jeremiah 31:31-35 Matthew 5:17, 26:28 Mark 14:24 Luke 22:20 1 Corinthians 5:3-4, 11:25 Romans 8:2-5, 11:26 Galatians 3:19 Hebrews 9:15-17, 10:10	2 Samuel 7:11b-16 1 Chronicles 17:10b-14 Psalm 89:36 Jeremiah 33:17 Luke 1:19, 26–33 Revelations 20–21

Four Covenants Woven Together (continued)

Name	Abrahamic	Mosaic	New Covenant	Davidic
Conditions	Unconditional	Conditional	Unconditional	Unconditional
Length	Eternal	Temporary	Eternal	Eternal
Parties involved	God and Abram	God and Moses	God promises physical blessings to the House of Israel and the House of Judah. The New Testament promises spiritual blessings to all those with faith in Christ.	David
Promises to	Descendants of Abraham through Isaac and Jacob	Moses and his descendants	House of Israel and House of Judah	David and his descendants

Appointed Days

Appointed Day	Passover		Firstfruits	Pentecost or Feast of Weeks	Feast/Day of Trumpets	Day of Atonement	Feast of Booths or Tabernacles	Sabbath
	Passover	Unleavened Bread						
Hebrew Name	Pesach	Chag Hamotzi	Yom Habikkurim	Shavuot	Rosh Hashanah or Yom Teru'ah	Yom Kippur	Sukkot	Shabbat
Date	14 Nisan (End of March)	15–21 Nisan (Around April)	Sunday after first Sabbath after Passover	Fifty Days after Firstfruits (Lasts one day. The only feast with no specific date.)	1 Tishri (Mid-September)	10 Tishri (Late September)	15–21 Tishri (Near October)	Sabbath (Begins Friday Evening)
Description	Lamb's blood shed.	Home cleansed of leaven.	First harvest of barley dedicated to the Lord (sheaf offering).	Firstfruits of wheat (two loaves of leavened bread) were offered to the Lord.	Although not the new year on the Jewish calendar, it came to represent the new year.	Considered the most holy day on the Jewish biblical calendar. Today it is a day of repentence and prayer to atone for sin.	Fall harvest celebration. It is a day of rejoicing and living in booths.	Remember to keep the Sabbath day holy.

Appointed Days (continued)

Appointed Day	Passover		Firstfruits	Pentecost or Feast of Weeks	Feast/Day of Trumpets	Day of Atonement	Feast of Booths or Tabernacles	Sabbath
	Passover	Unleavened Bread						
Historical	Israel is delivered from Egypt's bondage because of lamb's blood on door post and lintel. Causes death to "pass over" their first born.	Remove leaven from home. Eat unleavened bread for seven days.	Celebrates the first of the spring barley harvest brought to the tabernacle or temple as an offering to the Lord. If God blessed them with this early harvest, they expected He would provide the harvest that summer as well.	An offering of wheat was made. It was a time of thanksgiving for the early harvest, knowing that these early fruits promised a later harvest in the fall.	This is the day when the people of Israel take stock of their spiritual condition and repent to ensure the upcoming year would be pleasing to God. It is believed Moses ascended Mount Sinai to receive the Commandments on this date.	On this day, once a year, the High Priest would enter the Holy of Holies to make atonement for himself and the nation.		After God created the heavens and the earth, He rested on the seventh day. Sabbath means rest. Sabbath begins at sunset on Friday and continues through sunset on Saturday (Shabbat).

Appointed Days (continued)

Appointed Day	Passover			Pentecost or Feast of Weeks	Feast/Day of Trumpets	Day of Atonement	Feast of Booths or Tabernacles	Sabbath
	Passover	Unleavened Bread	Firstfruits					
Scripture References	OT: Exodus 12–13; Leviticus 23:5 NT: John 1:29, 36; 1 Corinthians 5:7; Matthew 26:26–28	OT: Exodus 12:14–20; Leviticus 23:6–18 NT: 1 Corinthians 5:7–8	OT: Leviticus 23:9–14; Leviticus 2:14–16 NT: 1 Corinthians 15:20–23	OT: Leviticus 23:15–21; Deuteronomy 16:9–12 NT: Ephesians 1:13–14, 4:30; 1 Corinthians 5:18–27; 12:12–13; Galatians 5:22–23; Acts 2	OT: Leviticus 23:23–25; 26:27–33; Numbers 10:1–10; Deuteronomy 28:58–67; Isaiah 11:1–12, 27:12–13; Ezekiel 36:24 NT: 1 Corinthians 15:51–53	OT: Leviticus 16:29–34, 17:11, 23:26–32; Numbers 29:7–11; Ezekiel 36:25–27; Zechariah 3:9; 12:10 NT: Hebrews 2:17–18, 3:1, 7–10, 9:19–22	OT: Leviticus 23:33–44; Deuteronomy 16:13–17; Zechariah 14:16–19 NT: 2 Corinthians 6:14–18; Matthew 25:21; 2 Timothy 4:1, 8; 2 Peter 3:3–13; Revelation 20:4–6	OT: Genesis 2:1–2; Exodus 20:8 NT: Mark 2:27

Appointed Days (continued)

Appointed Day	Passover		Firstfruits	Pentecost or Feast of Weeks	Feast/Day of Trumpets	Day of Atonement	Feast of Booths or Tabernacles	Sabbath
	Passover	Unleavened Bread						
Prophetical	Jesus died. His blood was shed. Jesus Christ is the Passover Lamb. No more sacrifices are needed.		Christ was resurrected as firstfruit on this day, promising that we would follow. He is the firstfruits to rise from the dead (1 Corinthians 15:20).	The promise of the Holy Spirit. The mystery of the Church: Jews and Gentiles in one body. On the first Day of Pentecost, 3,000 Jews responded to salvation and received the Holy Spirit.	Israel will be regathered in preparation for the final day of atonement.	All Israel will repent and be saved in one day.	Families will come to Jerusalem to celebrate Sukkot in the millennial kingdom. God will dwell with His people.	Sabbath means spiritual rest. Man rests from his own works if he has entered into God's rest (Hebrews 4:9–10).

161

Appointed Days (continued)

Appointed Day	Passover			Pentecost or Feast of Weeks	Feast/Day of Trumpets	Day of Atonement	Feast of Booths or Tabernacles	Sabbath
	Passover	Unleavened Bread	Firstfruits					
Symbolical	**Wine** represents the blood of Christ that was shed. **Bitter herbs** represent the struggles and tribulations that God's saints will experience in this life.	Leaven represents sin. Unleavened bread represents Christ's body, which is without sin.	Grain grown from the earth was lifted up high for everyone to see. Yeshua likens Himself to that grain in John 12:23–24.	The firstfruits are symbolic of God's spiritual kingdom. The firstfruits of believers at Shavuot guranteed a revival in the latter-day spiritual harvest for Messiah.	There will be a regathering in the last days of the remnant of believers. (Matthew 24:31). The shofar is symbolic of the hope that every believer possesses...the appearing of Messiah (Titus 2:13).	Messiah was our sacrifice.	The booth (sukkah) represents God dwelling with men. Messiah will dwell with His people.	Sabbath (Shabbat) is a symbol of rest that is continued throughout the New Testament. Sabbath was made for man (Mark 2:27).
				Fulfilled in Jesus	Yet to be Fulfilled			

Historical Timeline for Israel

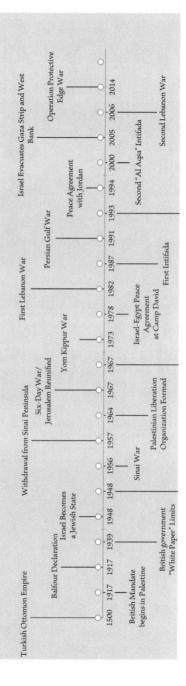

ACKNOWLEDGEMENTS

A huge thanks to the James L. Stamp Foundation who
generously provided a grant to publish this book.

A shout out to Linda Gilman, who not only prayed through the
preparation of the entire book, but edited it not once, but twice!

Thank you, Messianic Rabbi Doug Friedman, Robb Schwartz, and
Laurie Ruwe, for helping with the editing on some of the chapters.

Much appreciation to Ray Hart who donated his
talent and willingly illustrated the book.

To all those who are involved in our Bible studies and those involved
with Song for Israel—thank you for your encouragement and prayers!

To my parents, Jim and Shirley Callen, who introduced
me to my faith in Yeshua, encouraged me in writing and
teaching, and prayed throughout this project.

And to God, who prompted this writing and walked
me through each and every step along the way.

BIBLIOGRAPHY

Resources used to write this book are listed below by section to coincide with the four parts of the book.

Part One: Biblical Israel

Bennett, Todd D. *Walk in the Light: Covenants*. Herkimer, New York: Shema Yisrael Publications, 2014.

Chumney, Edward. *The Seven Festivals of the Messiah*. Shippensburg, Pennsylvania: Destiny Image Publishers, 1994.

Fruchtenbaum, Arnold G. *Israelology: The Missing Link in Systematic Theology*. San Antonio, Texas: Ariel Ministries, Inc., 1994.

Jones, Timothy P., David Gunderson, and Benjamin Galan. *Rose Guide to End-Times Prophecy*. Torrance, California: Rose Publishing, Inc., 2011.

Lenard, Joseph and Donald Zoller. *The Last Shofar!: What the Feasts of the Lord Are Telling the Church*. Salem Publishing Solutions, Inc. 2014.

Nadler, Sam. *Messiah in The Feasts of Israel*. Revised edition. Charlotte, North Carolina: Word of Messiah Ministries, 2010.

Ryrie, Charles Caldwell. *The Basis of the Premillennial Faith*. Revised edition. Dubuque, Iowa: ECS Ministries, 2005.

Saucy, Robert L. *The Church in God's Program*. Chicago: Moody Publishers, 1974.

Stern, David H. *Jewish New Testament Commentary: A companion Volume to the Jewish New Testament*. First edition. Clarksville, Maryland: Jewish New Testament Publications, 1992.

Teplinsky, Sandra. *Why Care About Israel? How the Jewish Nation Is the Key to Unleashing God's Blessings in the 21ˢᵗ Century.* Grand Rapids, Michigan: Chosen Books, 2004.

Teplinsky, Sandra. *Why STILL Care About Israel?.* Grand Rapids, Michigan: Chosen Books, 2013.

Part Two: Historical Israel

Arafat, Yasser. "The Impending Total Collapse of Israel." Speech at The Grand Hotel in Stockholm, Sweden, January 30, 1996.

Brog, David. *Standing With Israel: Why Christians Support the Jewish State.* Lake Mary, Florida: FrontLine, a Strang Company, 2006.

Gilbert, Martin. *Atlas of the Arab-Israeli Conflict.* New York, Oxford University Press, 1993.

Glick, Caroline B. *The Israeli Solution: A One-State Plan for Peace in the Middle East.* New York, Crown Forum, 2014.

"Netanyahu to Kerry: We want peace, but Palestinians continue to incite." *The Jerusalem Post.* November 6, 2013. http://www.jpost.com/Breaking-News/Netanyahu-to-KerryWe-want-peace-but-the-Palestinians-continue-to-incite-330763.

Prager, Dennis and Joseph Telushkin. *Why the Jews? The Reason for Anti-Semitism.* Simon & Shuster, 1983.

Prince, Derek. *The Key to the Middle East: Discovering the Future of Israel in Biblical Prophecy.* Minneapolis, Minnesota: Chosen, a division of Baker Publishing Group, 2013.

Richardson, Joel. *When A Jew Rules the World: What the Bible Really Says about Israel in the Plan of God.* World Net Daily (WND) Books, 2015.

Rydelnik, Michael. *Understanding the Arab-Israeli Conflict: What the Headlines Haven't Told You.* Chicago, Illinois: Moody Publishers, 2004.

Somfalvi, Attila. *Sanctions and suspended talks – Israel responds to Palestinian reconciliation.* Ynetnews.com, April 24, 2014.

Anti-Defamation League. "The Holocaust—Global Awareness and Denial." ADL Global 100, 2016. http://global100.adl.org/info/holocaust_info.

Anti-Defamation League. "Fight Anti-Semitism." https://www.adl.org/what-we-do/anti-semitism#.VbF0yP1VhBc

Arad, Uzi and Gal Alon. "Patriotism & Israel's National Security." Working paper, Institute for Policy & Strategy, Lauder School of Government, Diplomacy & Strategy, Herzliya, Israel, 2006.

"Boehner: Obama Administration's 'Animosity' toward Netanyahu 'reprehensible.'" *The Jerusalem Post*. March 29, 2015. http://www.jpost.com/Israel-News/Boehner-describes-Obama-administrations-animosity-towards-Netanyahu-as-reprehensible-395506.

"By the Numbers: The Holocaust." The National WWII Museum New Orleans. New Orleans, LA. http://www.nationalww2museum.org/learn/education/for-students/ww2-history/ww2-by-the-numbers/holocaust.html.

Dershowitz, Alan. "Are Israeli Settlements the Barrier to Peace?." Prager University video, 4:32. January 12, 2015. https://www.youtube.com/watch?v=dhbCtAz_BQc&feature=em-subs_digest.

The 50 Years War—Israel and the Arabs. Directed by David Ash and Dai Richards. Warner Bros., Brian Lapping Associates, and WGBH Educational Foundation, 1999. DVD.

Glick, Caroline B. *The Israeli Solution: A One-State Plan for Peace in the Middle East*. New York: Crown Forum, 2014.

Hafeez, Kasim. "Born to Hate Jews." Prager University video. 4:45. December 5, 2016. https://www.prageru.com/courses/political-science/born-hate-jews.

Israel 101 booklet, produced by StandWithUs. www.standwithus.com.

Jewish Virtual Library, www.jewishvirtuallibrary.org.

Saada, Tass. *Once An Arafat Man: The True Story of How a PLO Sniper Found a New Life*. Tyndale House Publishers, Inc. 2008.

Shapira, Anita. "The Past is Not a Foreign Country: The Failure of Israel's 'New Historians' To Explain War and Peace." *The New Republic*, November 29, 1999.

Teplinsky, Sandra. *Why Care About Israel? How the Jewish Nation Is the Key to Unleashing God's Blessings in the 21st Century*. Grand Rapids, Michigan: Chosen Books, 2004.

Teplinsky, Sandra. *Why STILL Care About Israel?*. Grand Rapids, Michigan: Chosen Books, 2013.

United Nations Relief and Works Agency for Palestine Refugees in the Near East, accessed April 26, 2017, www.unrwa.org.

United Nations Security Council, "Resolution 242." November 22, 1967.

Whiteman, Michele. "To the Media, Building Settlements in Israel's a Crime." *Huffington Post*, December 26, 2012. http://www.huffingtonpost. ca/michelle-whiteman/israeli-settlements-west-bank_b_2316941. html.

Part Four: Spiritual Israel

"Diversity." StandWithUs. http://standwithus.com/qr/diversity.html.

"Waves of Aliyah." International Christian Embassy Jerusalem. https://int. icej.org/aid/defining-aliyah.

"BDS: The Global Campaign to Delegitimize Israel." Anti-Defamation League. www.adl.org/education/resources/backgrounders/bds-the-global-campaign-to-delegitimize-israel-0.

Brown, Michael L. *Our Hands are Stained with Blood: The Tragic Story of the "Church" and the Jewish People*. Harrisburg, North Carolina: Destiny Image Publishers, Inc., 1990.

Buhler, Jurgen. "Jesus and the Palestinians." *Word From Jerusalem*, May 2014.

Glaser, Mitch. "A Painful Past." *Chosen People Ministries Newsletter*, June 2013, https://www.chosenpeople.com/site/newsletters/1306NL.

Glaser, Mitch. "President's Prayer Letter." February 2015. New York: Chosen People Ministries.

Langer, Walter C. "Hitler as His Associates Know Him," in *A Psychological Analysis of Adolph Hitler His Life and Legend*, The Nizkor Project.

http://www.nizkor.org/hweb/people/h/hitler-adolf/oss-papers/text/
oss-profile-03-02.html.

Melnick, Olivier. "The Six Dangers of Christian Palestinianism." Fight the
New Antisemitism, March 25, 2015. http://www.newantisemitism.
com/antisemitism/the-six-dangers-of-christian-palestinianism.

Melick, Olivier. *They Have Conspired Against You: Responding to the New
Anti-Semitism*, Huntington Beach, California: Purple Raiment, 2007.

Shaw, Berry. "Original thinking: When Israel Supporters use the Language
of Delegitimization." *The Jerusalem Post*, April 7, 2014. http://www.jpost.
com/printarticle.aspx?id=347822.

Stern, David H. *Jewish New Testament Commentary: A companion Volume to
the Jewish New Testament*. First edition. Clarksville, Maryland: Jewish
New Testament Publications, 1992.

Teplinsky, Sandra. *Why Care about Israel? How the Jewish Nation is the Key
to Unleasing God's Blessings in the 21ˢᵗ Century*. Grand Rapids, Michigan:
Chosen Books, 2004.

Wilkinson, Paul R. *For Zion's Sale: Christian Zionism and the Role of John
Nelson Darby*. Nittingham, England: Paternoster, 2007.

INDEX

A

Abrahamic Covenant 20, 25, 26, 27, 29, 34, 35, 75, 134, 143
Aliyah 135, 144, 145, 146, 170
Antichrist 151, 152
Anti-Defamation League 105, 106, 139, 140, 141, 169, 170
Anti-Semitism xv, 15, 99, 105, 128, 135, 136, 137, 138, 139, 140, 141, 142, 143, 144, 145, 147, 148, 149, 153, 168, 169, 171
Apartheid 99, 103, 104, 105, 127, 142, 143
Appointed Days 18, 51, 61, 70, 71, 72, 165. *See* Feasts
    Day of Atonement 52, 63, 66, 67, 68, 69, 70, 72, 158, 161
    Feast of Booths (Feast of Weeks) 52, 68, 158
    Feast of Firstfruits 58, 59, 72
    Feast of Trumpets 62, 63, 64, 65, 66, 71
    Feast of Unleavened Bread 52, 55, 57
    Passover 10, 31, 52, 53, 54, 55, 56, 57, 61, 72, 158, 161

    Pentecost 52, 54, 59, 61, 72, 158, 161
    Sabbath 18, 51, 52, 58, 70, 71, 158, 159, 161, 162
Arab 78, 79, 80, 82, 83, 85, 86, 87, 88, 89, 90, 92, 93, 103, 104, 105, 108, 110, 111, 112, 115, 117, 118, 119, 120, 122, 168, 169
Arafat, Yasser 89, 90, 92, 93, 118, 168
Assyria 120

B

Babylon, Babylonian 128
Balfour Declaration 78, 80
BDS 104, 136, 140, 153, 170
Blessing 20, 23, 25, 27, 29, 41, 46, 49, 52, 67, 70, 102, 120, 124, 127, 131, 138, 153, 156, 157, 168, 170, 171
Boycotts xiii, 104, 136, 140, 147, 153
British Mandate 78, 83, 102, 110, 129
Byzantine Empire 11

C

Camp David Summit 89, 90
Catholic 11, 18, 139

Gentile 5, 8, 9, 18, 24, 29, 30, 31, 32, 37, 38, 41, 42, 43, 44, 45, 47, 48, 49, 52, 60, 61, 70, 129, 130, 152, 156, 161

Gethsemane 39, 40, 41

Glaser, Mitch (author) xi, xiii, 7, 132, 133, 135, 138, 140, 148, 149, 170

Glick, Caroline (Israeli journalist) 122, 168, 169

God xi, xii, xiii, xv, 1, 2, 3, 4, 5, 7, 8, 9, 11, 14, 17, 18, 19, 20, 21, 22, 23, 24, 25, 26, 27, 28, 29, 30, 31, 32, 33, 35, 37, 41, 42, 43, 44, 45, 46, 47, 48, 49, 51, 52, 53, 54, 56, 57, 58, 59, 60, 61, 62, 63, 67, 68, 69, 70, 71, 72, 75, 109, 118, 119, 120, 124, 127, 128, 129, 130, 131, 132, 133, 134, 135, 138, 144, 145, 146, 147, 148, 149, 151, 152, 153, 154, 156, 157, 159, 161, 162, 165, 167, 168, 170, 171

God's Word 2, 8, 46, 59, 71, 133, 134, 135, 147, 148, 151

Gospel 8, 18, 23, 24, 130, 147, 148, 149

Grafting 43, 44, 45

H

Hamas 90, 93, 94, 104, 105, 117, 121, 123

Hate Speech 141, 142

Herzl, Theodor 77

High Priest 26, 63, 66, 67, 68, 159

Holidays 5, 18, 51, 52, 53, 148. *See* Feasts and Appointed Days
Chanukah 52, 53
Purim 53

Holocaust xiii, 16, 82, 83, 85, 99, 105, 106, 107, 108, 132, 140, 147, 169

I

Immigration 77, 82, 83, 138, 146

International Christian Embassy Jerusalem xi, 136, 145, 146, 153, 170

Intifada 89, 90, 94, 144

Islam 23, 79, 109

Israel 85, 94, 99, 100, 101, 102, 103, 104, 105, 108, 109, 110, 111, 112, 113, 115, 117, 118, 120, 121, 122, 123, 124, 127, 128, 129, 130, 131, 132, 133, 134, 135, 136, 137, 140, 142, 143, 144, 145, 146, 147, 148, 149, 151, 152, 153, 154, 156, 157, 159, 161, 163, 165, 167, 168, 169, 170, 171

J

Jacob 9, 29, 34, 35, 37, 42, 49, 75, 143, 145, 157

Jerusalem xi, xv, xvi, 10, 12, 34, 49, 51, 52, 54, 60, 70, 76, 84, 87, 89, 91, 94, 95, 99, 101, 103, 108, 109, 110, 117, 119, 121, 122, 136, 140, 142, 143, 145, 146, 151, 152, 153, 154, 161, 168, 169, 170, 171
Capital 88, 99, 108, 109, 110, 119, 143

Jesus xii, xv, 1, 7, 8, 9, 10, 16, 17, 18, 22, 24, 26, 29, 30, 31, 32, 33, 34, 35, 37, 38, 39, 40, 41, 42, 43, 46, 47, 48, 51, 52, 54, 56, 57, 58, 59, 61, 65, 67, 68, 71, 72, 109, 118, 127, 129, 130, 132, 133, 136, 140, 143, 147, 148, 149, 152, 161, 162, 170

Supersessionism 127